Mary E Herbert

Life of J. Theophane Venard, Martyr in Tonquin

What love can do

Mary E Herbert

Life of J. Theophane Venard, Martyr in Tonquin
What love can do

ISBN/EAN: 9783741166389

Manufactured in Europe, USA, Canada, Australia, Japa

Cover: Foto ©Andreas Hilbeck / pixelio.de

Manufactured and distributed by brebook publishing software (www.brebook.com)

Mary E Herbert

Life of J. Theophane Venard, Martyr in Tonquin

LIFE OF
J. THÉOPHANE VÉNARD,

Martyr in Tonquin;

OR, WHAT LOVE CAN DO.

TRANSLATED FROM THE FRENCH BY
LADY HERBERT.

"Ne soyons pas Apôtres à demi!"—*Letter of M. Vénard to M. Dallet, September 26, 1853.*

London:
BURNS, OATES, & CO.,
17 & 18, PORTMAN STREET, AND 63, PATERNOSTER ROW.
MDCCCLXX.

TRANSLATOR'S PREFACE.

THE present number of the "Foreign Missionary Series" may be called the "Letters," rather than the "Life" of the Martyr; for the Life is, in reality, but the silver thread on which the pearls are strung. These letters, which, I feel, have sadly lost in the translation, are models, not only of good writing and delicate imagery, but of holy thoughts, of godly counsels, of inexpressible tenderness, and yet of courageous firmness. Théophane Vénard was no ascetic saint, trembling at every manifestation of human or natural feeling. He was eminently a tender and dutiful son; a most devoted and loving brother; an equally devoted and attached friend. Neither did he consider these warm affections incompatible with the great work to which he had given his life. Writing to one of his oldest friends, F. Dallet, then a missionary in India, we find him exclaiming, "I love you with a special and devoted attachment, and have a full belief and confidence that God does not disapprove of it, for it is in Him and for Him that our hearts have been united."

A little later he talks of these strong links of human friendship being "given him by God, that each soul might be helped upwards by mutual love in the heavenly race." His devotion to his sister, whom he calls "part of his very life," with whom he was "united in one heart and one mind," as a "second self," shines through every page of this touching and beautiful correspondence. She is the first thought of his boyish years, she is his last thought in death. Yet all this strong human love did not prevent his sacrificing every thing to God; leaving the home he loved so fondly, the sister he idolized, the family tie which bound him with what others might have considered iron links,— every thing, in fact, which made life dear,—when the voice of the Master called him to go forth from his people and his country into a strange and distant land, to preach His word and do His work, and save the souls for whom He died upon the Cross. This is the striking characteristic of the life before us—human love, surpassing all ordinary home affections, willingly and joyfully offered up on the altar of our Lord for the salvation of the heathen who knew Him not.

The result of his labours and those of his companions, as detailed in the few simple pages before us, affords an abundant answer to those who talk of the failure of foreign missions in general, and of those of China in particular. In the western district alone of Tonquin, during the Episcopate of Mgr. Retord (the devoted Bishop under whom our holy Martyr laboured for the ten short years allotted to him by the Great Master of the vineyard), no less than *forty thousand* souls were added to the fold of Christ. The Ecclesiastical Seminaries he had established contained upwards of eighty native priests and one thousand two hundred catechists, while more than six hundred devout native women had enrolled themselves as sisters of charity, and powerfully seconded the efforts of the missionaries by their indefatigable labours. Of the fervour of the converts in the fulfilment of their religious duties, of the immense number of communicants (which are the real test of successful conversions), and of their constancy and courage in the confession of their faith amidst unheard-of tortures, there is incessant mention, not only in this little book, but throughout the Annals of the Propagation of the Faith.

It is more important than ever to impress the success of our Catholic Foreign Mission on people's minds, as, from the failure of other societies of the same name (especially that of New Zealand, which at one time was supposed to be so flourishing), men are apt to imagine that *all* missionary enterprizes are equal failures, and deserve neither encouragement nor support.

Without entering into the whole subject, let it suffice in this short Preface to inform our readers that in last year's Report of the "Séminaire des Missions Étrangères" at Paris, which, it must be remembered, is only one of the Colleges devoted to this Apostolic work, *one hundred and sixty-five thousand five hundred and twenty-one* souls were baptized in one year, of whom *eleven thousand six hundred* were adults; yet the operations of this Foreign Missionary College are confined to China and India.

It is further stated, from undeniable authority, that these numbers are daily increasing, in spite of the persecutions which, as in Tonquin and the Corea, threatened to annihilate the very name of Christian from the face of the earth.

So let us take heart and labour, each in our sphere, for this one end; remembering the words of our holy Martyr in his last letter written from his cage to his youngest brother:—

"As for us, if He gives us life, let us live for Him; if death, let us die for Him."

J. THÉOPHANE VÉNARD,

MARTYR IN TONQUIN.

CHAPTER I.

St. Loup-sur-Thouet is a little town in the department of the Deux-Sèvres, in the diocese of Poictiers, situated at some miles north of Parthenay, in a rich and deep valley. Here begins that beautiful golden valley which gives its name to the town of Airvault (*aurea vallis*), built in the shape of an amphitheatre, with its gothic church, and the ruins of an old castle. In spite of the ill-natured assertions of a modern author, the population of St. Loup is too serious and religious to have imbibed any Voltairian spirit. Even should it be true that the Author of the "Henriade" was born there, St. Loup now boasts of a more glorious hero. Thirty-five years ago, one of her citizens gave birth to a child who was to be not only the apostle of heathen nations, but the illustrious martyr whose life we are now about to write, and who has become the pride and the glory of his fellow-countrymen.

John Théophane Vénard, then, was born at St. Loup, on the 21st November, 1829, the day of

the Presentation of the Blessed Virgin. It was as
a foretaste of his tender devotion to our Mother; a
devotion which waxed stronger and stronger until
the hour of his sacrifice. He had the happiness to
belong to one of those patriarchal families now
becoming so rare amongst us, in whom religion and
honour hold the first place. His father, M. Jean
Vénard, whose family came originally from Anjou,
filled the post of village schoolmaster with as much
ability as devotion to his duties. He only gave up
this fatiguing post after thirty years of toil, to
accept the office of clerk of the peace in the district
of which the town of St. Loup was the capital.
There his experience in business, and his good
judgment, made him invaluable to his town's-
people until the day when his laborious and useful
labours were brought to a close.

His wife, Mme. Marie Guéret, was a gentle,
pious woman, simple and loving in character,
and devoting herself entirely to the care of her
own home. She had six children, two of whom
died as infants, but the others, Mélanie, Théophane,
Henri, and Eusèbe, will all play an important part
in this little history. Under the direction of these
good parents, the little Théophane made rapid
progress in all goodness and virtue. He combined
the loving, gentle character of his mother with the
firmness and resolution of his father; and when
first promoted to go to school with the other
children, he was already cited as a model of good
behaviour. Those who were his cotemporaries
still talk of the amusing contrast that existed
between his small, baby figure and his grave, quiet
manner. His greatest pleasure was to be allowed
to watch the goats or the cows on the hill-side, which
occupation fostered his love of solitude, and his
spirit of recollection. These hill sides and pleasant

fields hold an important place in the annals of the future missionary, for there the first thoughts of his ultimate vocation came upon him; and the feelings thus inspired remained among the sweetest of his whole life.

The country round St. Loup is very picturesque, but it owes its great fertility to the rivers, the Thouet and the Cebron, which intersect the valley in opposite directions. Between two beds of these two rivers is a hill-side called "Le Bel-Air," on account of its fresh and healthy situation, and the glorious view on all sides. When Théophane was only nine years old, his greatest delight was to pasture his father's goats on this spot with his sister or a mutual friend, and there they would sing, or read to each other books which they borrowed from the pastor of the village. Among these books, the "Annals of the Propagation of the Faith" had the greatest charm for the little boy. One day he was reading out-loud to his companions the life of the Venerable Charles Cornay, whose martyrdom was then recent. The account of the sufferings and death of this martyr for Jesus Christ touched him even to tears, and at last he cried out, "And I too will go to Tonquin, and I too will be a martyr!" A short time afterwards, his father joined them, and Théophane, turning to him with a gravity very unusual at his age, said, "Dear papa, how much is this field worth?" "Well, I really don't know exactly, my child," replied his father, "but why do you ask?" "Ah! because if you could give it to me, and I could have it for my share, I would sell it, and then I should be able to go to college, and study." His father, surprised at such serious thoughts in one so young, put him off with some simple answer; but he pondered over his words, which gave him a new light as to the character and intentions of his son. Soon after he allowed him to learn Latin with one or two other children who went for that purpose to the presbytery, and he succeeded so well in these first attempts that it was decided to send him to college, there to pursue a regular course of study.

At this time, the principal of the College of Doué, in the diocese of Angers, was a fervent and very superior man, and the brother of the venerable pastor of St. Loup.

It was to this college that young Vénard was sent in the month of October, 1841, together with a friend whom he had known and loved from a child. This friendship never cooled, and ten years after, Théophane wrote from Paris,—" Until I came to the Séminaire des Missions Étrangères, the only intimate friend I ever had was one who had been born in my own village, and who was dear to me as my own soul. The same fatherly hand baptized us; side by side we sat on our benches at school; and at the very same time we were transplanted together to a new home, where another father received us both with open arms. My friend was older, cleverer, and wiser than I, and took a higher place in the College, but our friendship was not the least affected by this. He flew, and I crawled; but we were each quite contented. I was transferred to the "Petit Séminaire;" and there we found each other again in the same cloister, sharing the same masters, the same studies, the same companions. God, who had united us in childhood, gave us but one thought, one aim, and one object in life. But the day at last came when we were to be separated—my life seemed to be broken altogether! But I have the firm hope that we shall be reunited in Heaven."

No sooner was he fairly established at college, than Théophane gave his whole mind to the fulfilment of his duties. He was a model to the other students, not only during the hours of study, but also during recreation, when he showed himself the gayest and most merry of the whole party. He bore all ill-nature or contradiction with such good humour that those who were at first inclined to tease him, soon gave it up. The more people had vexed him, or given him pain, the greater was his kindness towards them, and he rarely failed to win their hearts, and make them ashamed of their previous behaviour.

He gladly entered into all the little private devotions of the students, which were in harmony with his taste and affections. Even as a little child he had vowed a special devotion to the Blessed Virgin; and after his entrance into the College, on the Feast of the Immaculate Conception, he resolved to say his Rosary every week. A little later, he was inscribed among the children of Mary, at Notre Dame des Victoires, and enrolled himself in the work of the propagation of the faith, determined to help other missionaries as far as he could, until he became one himself. He tried also to lead, as much as he was permitted, a hard and mortified life; and on a winter's day, one of the masters, seeing him suffer very much from chilblains on his hands and feet, having asked him to warm himself by the comfortable fire in his room, Théophane refused, exclaiming, "The missionaries you were talking to us about last night, sir, suffered much more than that!"

He had a passion for reading, and delighted in the lives of children of his own age, and especially of those who had suffered martyrdom. All these holy dispositions were fostered by the thoughts of his first Communion, which was approaching; and for which, unlike the generality of boys, he prepared himself with the utmost anxiety and care.

"The day is almost come," he wrote to his parents, "that day which I have so earnestly desired! the most beautiful day in my whole life! Please pray to the Blessed Virgin for me, that I may receive her Son worthily, for I feel I can never prepare myself sufficiently for so solemn an occasion. I beg of you, therefore, to forgive me any faults I may have committed against you, and to give me your blessing."

Great as had been his previous doubts and fears, when the time came, his joy knew no bounds. "I remember him perfectly on that day," wrote one of his tutors. "He seemed not able to contain himself for happiness." From that hour began his great devotion to the Blessed Sacrament. He would often steal away to visit It during times of recreation. "I often used to open the door of the chapel softly to see if he was there," wrote the same master, "and was always edified by his wonderful spirit of recollection. I used sometimes to force him to go out, to make him play with his companions, which I thought necessary for his health, and then devotion gave place to instant obedience."

But a great sorrow was hanging over his head, for which Théophane would need all the strength his Lord had vouchsafed to him in the Sacrament of His love. After two happy months spent with his family, he was forced to part with his mother to return to college, and he foresaw that their parting would be a final one. Very soon after, in fact, she expired calmly in the arms of her husband, leaving him the care of their four little children. The blow to Théophane was terrible. Nevertheless, his first thought was how he could best console the mourners at home.

"Dearest papa," he writes, "when you wrote me word that my darling mother was very weak and suffering, I flattered myself that our prayers and tears would win from God the preservation of her life. But just now the head-master has told me of the terrible misfortune which has befallen us. O my God, enable me to say, Thy Will be done! The hour fixed by Him was at hand, and she has had to leave us, and is gone to be our protector in Heaven with the two little angels to whom she gave birth. Oh, once more, may His Holy Name be blessed! It is thus He tries His creatures here below. Putting on the buckler of faith, we will have recourse to religion, which alone can comfort us in such sorrows. But it is very, very bitter. I have cried till I can cry no longer, and I have prayed with all my heart for her dear soul. May she at this moment be in the enjoyment of the Beatific Vision with His elect! May the Saviour, whom she ever loved and strived to serve, have received her into His kingdom."

But our Lord reserved to this holy child a special consolation. Many years after the event, and at the moment when he was about to leave his family for ever, he broke silence on the subject, and said, "I think I may assure you positively that our good mother is in Heaven. I tell you this for your comfort; but I have never spoken of it before, and I must beg of you not to repeat it to any one. At the time of her death, one night when I was watching in prayer, an angel took me by the hand and led me, as it were, into a great and wonderful Light, in the midst of which, surrounded by other glorified bodies, I distinctly saw her whom we so fondly loved, and for whom we had wept so bitterly." From the time of this great sorrow the links which bound the brother and sister together were drawn closer, and a correspondence began between Théophane and Mélanie, which only ceased with death. Their letters remain as models of tenderness and holy inspirations, while they are unexceptionable in point of style and taste. Speaking on this subject, Mgr. De Poictiers says, "It is in this outpouring of heart to heart that we see his extreme delicacy of feeling, his loving thoughtfulness, his graceful imagination, and the good judgment which balanced all his other qualities. We have read these letters again and again with ever-increasing pleasure, and we trust we shall be forgiven if we have watered some of them with our tears."

In the course of the winter of 1844, Théophane writes, "I must send you a few lines, my dearest sister, for there is not a day, nor scarcely an hour, when I do not think of you, who are so very dear to me. I know you too are thinking of me, and I daresay you will be saying, 'Oh, my poor old brother will be so cold this winter; and here am I enjoying a good big fire!' Be comforted; though I have suffered from the cold, as you know I always do, yet I have had some fun out of it too, for we have had famous skating. And now the weather is milder, and I am thawing, and pouring out some of my thoughts to my second self."

Soon after, his brother Henry joined him at the College; and it was impossible not to be touched at the care he took of him, and the way he watched over him, so as to spare him the usual schoolboy troubles. In 1845, the confraternity of the Children of Mary was established in the College, which Théophane announced with joy to his sister. He was made Sacristan of his chapel, an honour which he greatly coveted, as not only it gave him the care of the altar, but it enabled him to steal away oftener for prayer. "Yesterday," he wrote to Mélanie, "I went to say my rosary in the chapel; and I don't know why, but I was very sad, and I began to cry like a child; but all the time I had a wonderful kind of interior consolation, and every thing appeared to me in a supernatural light. . . . Very often, when I am at work, my thoughts fly back to you. I seem to see you going lightly about the house, singing softly as is your wont, and doing things for our father and the children and every body. I follow you in thought every where. Although so far apart, our thoughts, our wishes, our aspirations seem to be one. Oh, what a blessed thing it is, this communion of soul, to be able to pray for each other, and to pray for our loved ones together! A sort of peace and calm comes over me then. Do you know, the other day, on the Feast of our Patron Saint, at Benediction, kneeling before the Blessed Sacrament, the Blessed Virgin seemed to smile amidst her flowers and tapers, and I thought of you, who I know were then at the vespers of the confraternity. I prayed so hard for you, and I felt you were doing the same for me, and as if our prayers were one. And then I felt so happy, so relieved. But I should like to be with you again in body as well as in spirit. Oh, when shall we cease to be separated? When shall we be able to live together as we did as children, and share all our troubles and all our joys?"

It seemed as if a vision of the future were before him—that future which was to be so great a struggle to flesh and blood. But we must not anticipate.

On New Year's Eve, 1847, he wrote to his father:—

"Here we are in the midst of piercing frost and cold; but if the winter numbs our limbs, at least it does not freeze our hearts. Whatever happens— whether my chilblains disappear or not—I can't let New Year's Day pass without scribbling a few lines to repeat once more to you my hearty prayers and wishes for your happiness. People declare that New Year's Day is the day for telling lies. Let those say so who tell them. As for me I always welcome the return of the anniversary as an occasion for renewing the expressions of my old childhood's love. In one word, dearest papa, I wish you many, many happy New Years."

At this time Théophane was eighteen. In spite of having given himself up to God from his youth, the devil filled him with doubts and temptations, when it came to a question of deciding on his future vocation, and, as usual, his sister is the *confidante* of his troubles:—

"My dearest Mélanie,—We must talk a little of the Blessed Virgin, for I feel as if I had not spoken enough of her this year. Can it be that I have changed? I think not; but other thoughts preoccupy me just now. I am nearly at the end of my classes here, and yet I seem to have no clear conception of my future. This worries me very much. I always thought I was called to the priesthood. Sometimes I say to myself, 'What a glorious thing it is to be a priest!' 'What it would be to be able to say one's first Mass!' But then for that one must be so good!—so pure!—like one of God's angels. That is why I still hesitate. Please to unite your prayers with mine, that I may discern God's will in the matter. Will you? But why do I ask? I know you will, and I want you to give me your communion the first Sunday in Lent with this intention, and I will prepare myself for the same."

A little later he writes, "O my dearest sister, do write to me at once, for I look to you only for comfort. Bring back hope to my poor sad heart; that is your mission, you know. As regards me, I should like to laugh and be merry with you; but I have not the heart. I wait for your letter with the greatest anxiety."

Still his heart turned towards Mary in the midst of his greatest distresses: "O Mary, how I love the word! Mary, refuge of sorrowful hearts! Mary, under whose wing we have both sheltered ourselves, like little children with their mother at the approach of the enemy. I love Mary, but I think you, my dearest sister, love her more." . . . Then he comes back to his previous sorrow. "I get so weary of life and of every thing, I don't know what to do. It is only to you that I dare own such a thing. But you, you are half of myself. You are more than my sister—you are my guardian angel."

At last, by God's grace, peace came back to his soul, and he writes,—

"Dearest Mélanie,—Thank you, my good little sister, thank you a thousand times for your delicious letter. Oh what good it has done me! Once more I thank you with all my heart, that's all I can say. Here is the month of Mary nearly over! it is high time we should talk about her a little. We too have special devotions every day for Mary's month, and I delight in decorating her altar. We have a quantity of beautiful roses in the garden here. The largest and sweetest, you may be sure, I keep for our tender, good Mother, and it is a great pleasure to offer her fresh ones every morning. I fear the hands and the heart that bring them are miserably unworthy; but she is so good, she receives every body! Well may we call her the 'Comfort of the Afflicted,' and the 'Refuge of Sinners.'

"Oh, if you did but know how my poor old head works when I am all alone, and can't sleep for thinking! Oh, how happy I should be in a quiet country parish with my Mélanie! I would guide the good people to try and save their souls, and you would have care of the church; and together we would labour for God, and talk of Him and of His Mother, and of all those we have loved and lost. But one thought troubles me in the midst of all these castles in the air. All this is very good and very pleasant certainly; but when it comes to the point, what is the Priesthood? Is it not the entire detachment from all worldly goods—a complete abandonment of all temporal interests? To be a Priest, one should be a Saint. To guide others, one must first learn to guide oneself. Then should not the life of a good Priest be one of continual sacrifice, self-immolation, and mortification of all kinds? How in the world should I ever have the courage to embrace such a life,—I that am so little advanced in the paths of virtue, or of penance?

"These are my thoughts, darling sister, and they always come back to the same.

"But when I pray to God to enlighten me, I seem to hear an interior voice ever singing, 'Thou must be a Priest;' 'God gives His grace to all who ask Him.' Then a great peace seems to come over me, and I find myself happy and contented. You will say, 'What on earth am I to conclude from all this?' Why, that the choice of a vocation is a terrible thing, and that whoever thinks of it seriously is in a desperate difficulty.

"But as far as concerns myself, I hope, in spite of my unworthiness, that God will have pity upon me. Our God is likewise a Father, and that a most tender Father; and we have besides a powerful Advocate in one who deigns to be our Mother." But in Mélanie's own heart the struggle was going on likewise as to the choice of a vocation, and the mutual difficulties and the entire confidence they had in each other, bound them, if possible, still more closely. In Théophane's mind his sister appeared more and more holy, while his own love to our Lord increased in the like proportion.

He writes again to her, "You may be quite sure that I am true to my promise, and if you pray for me I feel sometimes as if my life were one prayer for you. But though you will laugh at me for saying so, I can't help sometimes, when I am asking God and His saints to enlighten us, I can't help, I say, wishing for what you do not desire. I hear you say, 'But this is not right; this is not really loving me.' Don't be angry, the thought is repented of as soon as conceived. But the fact is, I cannot bear the idea of a total separation. I am afraid this arises from egotism on my part; never mind, it is only a slight shade. No, dearest Mélanie! believe this, that I will never try for an instant to turn you from any generous or holy project. I should be afraid of robbing you of your crown! But I tell you frankly that to lose you would be a terrible sacrifice on my part. Every time the thought comes across me, I beg for the grace of God to enable me to bear it, if it be His will that you should go and leave us. I only wish for your highest happiness. You say that God calls you. If so, so much the better for you! I can only envy your lot, and hope that some day I may have the like favour. Let us leave to our dear Lord and Master to direct our future: our only business is to strive to correspond to His grace as far as we possibly can."

But Théophane was going upwards with rapid strides, and not content with the Priesthood, was beginning to thirst after the higher glories of the Apostolate. He said himself later that he was, as it were, led by the hand, without knowing whither he was going. The following little memorandum, found among his copy-books, and dated 17th June, 1847, shows the working of his mind at that time :—

"To-day in the chapel of the College at Doué, I made a vow to Mary, Refuge of Sinners, to say my Rosary every day, *in order to obtain a special grace from God.*"

In the following letter to his sister, he gives an enthusiastic description of the procession on the Festival of Corpus Christi, and concludes with the words, " If religious services on earth are so glorious, what must they be in Heaven ? Eternity! have you ever thought of this word ? Eternal, Eternal, Eternal! a thing which will never, never end. Thinking on such subjects sometimes overwhelms me, although I am still inclined to be giddy and thoughtless. I try sometimes to make some sort of theory about it which I can comprehend ; but when I have made my plan I only feel, 'Oh what a goose I am !' and then all my fine building crumbles away."

Théophane had remained six years at the College of Doué, and already gave promise of great ability. His frank, sweet-tempered nature made him a universal favourite, while his piety, sound judgment, and high principle won the respect and confidence of his tutors. Although kind towards every one, he cared but for his own family and for two or three of his companions; but on these he lavished all the wealth of his affectionate, loving heart. This devotion to his family and to one or two congenial souls far exceeded any ordinary love or friendship, and seemed to be permitted by God in order to show the full power of His grace, which hereafter would wean him from all human ties, and say to him, as to Abraham, "Go forth out of thy country, and from thy kindred, and out of thy father's house, and come into the land which I shall show thee."

As to his personal appearance, although under the middle height, he had a peculiarly pleasing and taking appearance, with a frank expression, a clear complexion, bright eyes, and a very fascinating manner. He was above the average in his studies, always bringing home the first prizes; and he had a great talent for poetry and other kinds of composition. At the vacation in 1847 he left school, and in the month of October entered what is called "Le Petit Séminaire" at Montmorillon. He was immensely happy here, and wrote to his sister, "From the bottom of my heart, dearest Mélanie, I do assure you I never was so happy. . . . *Cor unum et anima una*, this is the motto of the congregation! Such words can only come from God Himself! Is not that the link which united all Christians to each other? Is it not this feeling which creates the Missionary, the Priest, the Christian Brother, the Sister of Charity. *Cor unum*, we can apply it to ourselves, for our love and our hopes are one. Oh, yes. *Cor unum et anima una!* We can say so now, and we shall be able to say so still better later, if God calls you to serve Him more distinctly. Go, go, my dear, good sister, I will never stop you, notwithstanding the sorrow I cannot help feeling at the idea. But think a little bit of our father, our dear, good old father. I pray for you every day, that God may deign to enlighten us both, and show us His Holy Will."

There was nothing gloomy or repelling in his religion. On the contrary, he was always cheerful and merry, but especially at Montmorillon, where his *entrain* and gaiety became proverbial, and the little feasts of which he was the presiding genius will be remembered as long as his generation remains.

In spite of his gaiety and fun, however, Théophane had a strong groundwork of serious and deep feeling, which came out in his letters to his little brother, of which we will give some extracts here:—

"MY DEAR LITTLE EUSEBIUS,—Well, how do you like school? Are the lessons very hard? very disagreeable? Courage! you are just now at the bottom of the ladder. Very soon you will get on, and see the fruit of your work. Have you found any fellows that you like? have you jolly games together? Tell me all. I so often think of my poor little brother, and wish I could be with him, especially in these first weeks of his school life. . . It is half-past six in the evening. The wind blows through the chinks of the door; isn't it bitter? But I feel so for you, my poor little man. I am sure your poor little toes and paws are all over chilblains, as mine used to be; and the tip of your nose is all frozen, isn't it? Ah! but that's the true life of a schoolboy! We go to learn to bear; but let us leave the winter behind, and wish one another a very, very happy New Year, and Paradise by and by, though I hope not just yet, as I don't feel disposed to give up my little brother so soon. I recollect in old times how you used to long for

New Year's Day, but then that was for all the presents and sugar-plums. Now, alas! there are no presents and no goodies—only lessons. Oh, dear! But by and by you will be glad to have learned something, so as to be more fit to fulfil the duties God will appoint for you in life, and so win Heaven. For that, dear Eusebius, and that alone, must be the object of all our actions. Work hard, work well, not to get praise, or honour, or prizes, but because you will thus please God. Take this as the maxim of your life: '*All for our good God.*' Don't neglect your prayers. Be docile to your superiors, for they are set over you by God; be loving and kind to your companions, and then every body will love you, and you will be really happy."

Then came his little brother's first Communion, and Théophane writes,—

"My dear little brother has just made a great step in life, and a step towards another world. For one little moment you paused and pitched your tent, and looked back to all your childish faults, faults which the world counts little, but which a Christian judges of differently; and kneeling at the foot of God's priest, you have told him of all these little failings and shortcomings, and he has lifted off the burden from your shoulders with the words of absolution in the name of the Thrice Holy God. You have become once more innocent as a little child, and the friend of the angels; and you have received Him whom the heaven of heavens cannot contain. Oh, the inexpressible happiness of the child's first Communion! Who can describe that mystery of love? Only angels know that language. May you understand it, too, my dear little angel on earth!"

Théophane was now eighteen; his year of philosophy was over, and he was about to be transferred from the "Petit" to the "Grand Séminaire," but first he was allowed to go home, and his joy found vent in the following words:—

"In a month more I shall see the sky of my native valley; how happy the thought makes me! My friends at the 'Grand Séminaire' begin their vacation a month sooner, which makes me rather envious. Well, the time will soon slip by. My schoolboy life is at an end; it has not been without its trials, but it has had its sweets too. *For the moment* I feel as if I wanted the fresh air of my own dear home to strengthen me, body and soul. Till now I have not *lived*, so to speak. Now I am going to begin. Every living thing seems to me to follow its vocation. The river flows to the sea, and the plant germinates, and the animal feeds and grows, and man lives and draws daily nearer to God. But each man walks after his own fashion. The business of one is to cultivate the soil; another, the intellect. Handicrafts supply the material wants of mankind; politics, the social. One and all gravitate towards their end, which is death, although each follows a different path. In one sense man has a free will, but he can scarcely be said to choose his career; it is almost always marked out for him. If he wanders from it, nothing but confusion is the result. Well, I am longing to work and to find my place in the world, to spend and be spent for my brethren. Whatever course be proposed to me, I always come back to that—*to be a Priest*. No other career has the least attraction for me. Yes, one day I shall be the soldier of Jesus Christ, and fight under the banner of the Church, and the day will soon dawn for the fulfilment of that wish. That is why I feel so happy at the thought of going home so soon. A week or two among my own people, and then to my cell and to my vocation for evermore."

CHAPTER II.

Théophane Vénard entered the "Grand Séminaire," as we have seen, with the firm determination to become a Priest. He understood at once how important the training there given would be to him; and the shortness of the time allowed made him grasp at every opportunity to improve himself, especially as regarded his sanctification. With a clear and subtle intellect, and abilities very much above the common, he at once distinguished himself among his companions; but none of these qualities made him lose sight of the great virtue of humility, which he cultivated assiduously, so as always to try and escape notice by burying himself among the rest. He also made charity act as the handmaid of humility; and therefore not only refrained from any unkind act or word, but denied himself many of those little sharp and amusing "repartees" which his wit and sense of fun made often very tempting to him; preferring to pass for one who was dull and could not enter into a joke, than to wound in the smallest degree the feelings of another. "I do not think this was the least remarkable of his virtues," wrote one of his college friends, who is now a Dominican.

His regularity in his work attracted the attention of all his masters; and he even began to have a sort of scruple as to the length of his letters to his family. His cell was his delight, and he realized the promises in the "Imitation" towards those who jealously guard their little sanctuary.

"Every thing speaks to me in my cell," he writes to his sister. "I love it as a mother loves her child. Every thing about it encourages me to charity and devotion. I come in; to the right is my holy water stoup, and it seems to say to me, 'Your cell is your sanctuary: nothing impure must enter it,' and so I leave my worldliness at the door, and purify myself with holy water. I walk towards the window, and look out on the sky, and I say to myself, 'Up there a place is reserved for you ; work and struggle hard to win it.' Then I beg of our Lord to bless my labour, and lest any strange thought should disturb my mind, there hangs my Crucifix, preaching for ever by the Divine example. Then above my book-case, the Cross stretches out its arms and covers me with its shadow ; and soon I shall have also the picture of Mary immaculate watching over her Child. You fancy that I may have some troubles in my present life, dear Mélanie ? No; I do assure you this place is to me a paradise upon earth. Every one is happy here, even those who, like me, are far from being saints!"

At the same time he was ever mindful of his home ties, and seized every little opportunity for opening his heart to his family. "How good you are to me!" he wrote one day, "and how I love you for your tender thought of me! I said, 'I want some sleeves,' and in a trice here they are! 'I should like a curtain for my window,' and there it hangs, keeping out all curious eyes. I wanted some money, and behold, here it is, without my asking ! as well as half a dozen minor things which make my little establishment complete. Only one thing is lacking, and that is time! A little quarter of an hour to say, 'Thank you!' and again, 'Thank you!'"

On one occasion he describes to his family the departure of one of the students of the College for the Foreign Missions, and his secret wish for the first time broke forth: "Several vocations of the like nature have declared themselves," he exclaims. "It is quite glorious! We are in a state of excitement and enthusiasm about it not to be described." These words awoke some fears at home, especially in the heart of the sister who knew him best: and he writes in reply, "So my news troubled you, dear little sister, did it? But is there any thing so very extraordinary in one among us devoting himself to the salvation of the heathen? Why, one talks of going to be a Jesuit; another, to La Trappe; another to China; and so on! Oh, if you think there are no events and no gossip in the College, you are very much mistaken. But you have created a whole world of hope and fears out of that one little sentence of mine! I can scarcely help laughing. Another time don't let your imagination run wild, but sleep in peace."

In this humble and hidden life, like that of his Master at Nazareth, nothing is so striking as the way he passed from the natural to the supernatural. Every thing spoke to him of God. One day after telling his brother how at Easter he had changed his room, and altered the arrangement of his things, he adds, "It is quite an event for me, this change; and now I am going to work away with fresh courage, for one thought pursues me, and seems to me to be at the bottom of all one's college life.

"Why have I come here?" *Ad quid venisti?* Why come to a theological seminary? It is to go through a certain course of instruction, you will say. Well, but that course comes to an end; *and then?* ... Oh, when that thought comes across me, I simply bow my head, and beg of God to answer me. I will do as He shall appoint."

The ceremonies and anniversaries of the Church as celebrated in the College impressed him strongly, and were the constant subjects of his letters. On Good Friday he was specially moved, and wrote as follows :—

"Oh, this is indeed a sad and exceptional day at the college! ... To see us all mournfully wandering here and there in the cloisters, without a sound being heard, not a voice, not even a whisper, one would imagine we were sheep without a shepherd. And it is quite true: the Pastor of pastors is dead; the Pastor has given His life for His sheep."

These pious thoughts, which seemed to come naturally to the young theological student, were often poured out to his brother and sister. With his younger brother especially it seemed to him the best and most delicate way of making him take an interest in serious things without disgusting him by lectures, or appearing to be always "preaching" to him. "I like to think of you on all these occasions," he wrote one day, "and I fancy I see you, so recollected in prayer, so studious in class, so merry and gay at recreation, and making us all so glad and happy! for to be good is to be happy; and we cannot be thoroughly happy unless you are the same."

In the faithful practice of all these relative duties, Théophane made the best preparation for the priesthood. The Christmas ordination, at which he had only assisted as a spectator, had touched him to the quick. When the Trinity one came round, he was desired to prepare himself for the first step by receiving the tonsure.

"My dearest Sister," he writes, "to-morrow I am to be tonsured; that is, I shall no longer belong to the world, but to our Lord. I shall say to Him, 'My God, Thou art the portion of my heritage, and of my lot. Thou wilt give me a place in Thy heavenly Kingdom.' I shall say to the Blessed Virgin, '*Regina cleri, ora pro nobis!*' Oh how proud I shall be to wear on my head the crown of the saints! that crown to obtain which it would not be too much to devote one's whole life!" But his happiness was to be delayed some time longer, owing to the death of the beloved bishop of the diocese. In so public a calamity, his generous soul could not think for a moment of a personal disappointment which had been swallowed up in the general mourning. Just before the long vacation his father's feast-day came round; and in spite of the press of work before the Examinations, he found time to write a few loving words: "My dearest Father,—I try to fancy myself with you on Saturday evening, and embrace you with all my heart, while offering you the flower which most expresses my humble but devoted love. O Thou who art the Master of life and death, preserve to us our darling father; watch over him, and keep him in all his ways now and ever."

The first year of his college life was over, and it had been fruitful in gifts and graces. But always afraid of himself, and fearful lest he should relax during the long vacation, he wrote out a series of Resolutions, which we will give verbatim:—

A. M. G. D. July 1, 1849.

SOME RESOLUTIONS FOR THE HOLIDAYS.

One year of my college life is already past, and I must give an account of this time of retreat and sanctification. Alas! where are the graces which I have acquired? My God, Thou hast searched me out, and known me. Even the angels are not pure in Thy sight; and what am I? . . . . O my divine Redeemer, have mercy upon me. Deign to accept my penitence, and to bless the resolutions which, with the help of Thy grace, I hope to make for the future. Virgin Mother! thou who from my childhood I have chosen, pray for me, for thou art my refuge and my strength. "*Refugium peccatorum, ora pro nobis!*"

1. I will get up the moment I wake, offering my heart to Jesus and Mary. I will never get up later than six. If I serve the six o'clock Mass, I will say my prayers and the little hours afterwards. If the eight o'clock, then I will say them all before, together with my meditation and the study of a certain portion of Holy Scripture. The rest of the office I will say in the evening at separate times.

2. I will make a particular Examen every day before luncheon at two o'clock. This examination to consist of a few minutes' meditation on faith, charity, modesty, interior recollection, &c., &c., with a special consideration of the way in which I have practised each. At the end of the month I will make a general examination, to prevent my relapsing into laxity or indifference.

3. In the course of the afternoon or evening I will make a visit to the Blessed Sacrament, making use of St. A. Liguori's Exercises on the subject. I will also take for my meditation book the "*Me-*

moriale Vitæ Sacerdotalis" (by Claude Arvisenet), besides the "Imitation" and the Holy Scriptures, both of which I always carry with me.

4. Directly after breakfast I will spend an hour or so in working either at my holiday task or at the Holy Scriptures. In the evening, after Vespers and Compline, I will study again a little bit, but on less serious subjects. I could do this while walking, or when I am waiting at the Curé's.

5. In my intercourse with the outside world, I will try and be most careful in speech. I will be gentle and kind towards every one, and especially towards my own family. Should the occasion present itself, I will never neglect to say a little word of our good God, especially to the children. But I will do this with great caution, remembering that deeds are worth more than words.

6. On Feast days I will work between Mass and Vespers if I have time. On those days I will try and keep up a greater spirit of recollection.

7. Of all these Resolutions, there are one or two which I must strictly put into practice, such as prayer, the particular Examen, the visit to the Blessed Sacrament, and the spiritual reading of the "Imitation" or the "Memoriale."

Upon the other points I may be less severe; especially if my friends or companions insist upon my accompanying them in a walk or on a party of pleasure. In fact, I must be careful to do nothing singular or out of the way, so as to excite observation; all affectation, therefore, is *tabooed*. True merit is hidden and simple, and dreads nothing more than publicity. If I can only keep always humble, charitable, and modest, I may escape some of the dangers of my long vacation. I am sure good examples will not be wanting to me; and then, have I not the grace of God? "*Dominus custodiat te. Dominus protectio tua. Omnia possum in eo qui me confortat.*"

T. Vénard.

No mention is made in this little Rule of Life of the frequentation of the Sacraments or other devotions; but as he followed strictly the rule of the Seminary in all these points, it was not necessary to speak of them. No mention is made either of the Rosary. But as it was said every evening in his family circle, he presided at it during his holidays as a matter of course. Perhaps some of our readers may be surprised at his Rule being so simple, and with so few austerities. But it arose from his determination to keep it strictly, so that it should not be a dead letter. Moreover, he thought it right for the sake of those around him to share in their simple pleasures, and in the expeditions and picnics which took place during his visit. But his greatest delight was to be with his sister, and to talk with her of holy things and of their future vocations; and daily was the soul of each strengthened by their mutual intercourse.

Two months after his return to the Seminary (on the 8th of December), Mgr. Pie, the new Bishop of Poictiers, made his solemn entry into his episcopal town. The sight of this young and saintlike Bishop had a great effect on Théophane, and all the more as it ensured the Christmas ordination, when he was to receive the tonsure. From that moment he considered himself as set apart for the priesthood, and redoubled his zeal and fervour. At the Trinity ordination, in 1850, he received minor orders, and wrote to his father, "Oh what a grand day is that of one's Ordination! How I wish you had been here to share in my joy! But you will come, will you not, when the great and final step is taken?

You will add your blessing to the rest? Oh, it seems as if I could hardly wait patiently for the dawning of such a great day!"

The vacation came round again, and he took the opportunity to open his heart more entirely to his sister, both for his own consolation and because he knew that her faith would triumph over all human considerations, and help him to overcome the shrinkings of his loving heart as he thought over a separation which would probably be final. He spent almost the whole time at home, and employed part of it in helping his brother to make a little grass terrace at the foot of the garden, where, he fancied, after his departure, they would all be able to sit and think of the absent one whom they had freely given for God's work. On his return to college he seems to have redoubled his efforts to profit by this last year of study and preparation for his future career. But he did not neglect others in thinking of himself, and his letters to his little brother and to his sister are more frequent than ever. To the former he writes on the beauty of piety in the young, adding, however, "Now don't imagine it necessary to put on a sour face, or to look sanctimonious. True devotion is natural, gay, and bright, according to the words of St. Paul, '*Gaudete in Domino semper; iterum dico, gaudete.*'"

To his sister he writes more as to an equal.

"I rejoice, my darling Mélanie, to see you growing every day in fervour and the love of God. I am sure we shall both try and not forget that humility is the base of all perfection, and that obedience is its guardian. Do read Rodriguez's article on Humility in his work on Christian Perfection. But do not let this book give you any scruples, as it is addressed to nuns, and one must not confound absolute precepts with practices which vary according to the position and duties of each person. .... I quite understand what you say in your letters about the sacrifice hanging over our heads. But, courage! God only asks of us our good will; His grace does the rest. What I am most afraid of, is lest you should be discouraged. The Christian motto is Hope! Hope on! hope ever! Be very generous as regards our good God. Try and leave all things to Him, without trouble or preoccupation. 'In quietness and confidence shall be your strength.' If you feel you have been wanting in such feelings, make a little act of contrition, and then rise up again quickly with renewed courage. In this way we shall really feel as children of God in the holy liberty wherewith Christ has made us free. To be truly humble; to fly from this world's notice; to hold ourselves continually as in the presence of God; to be little in our own eyes,—these are the dispositions most pleasing to Him, and which are easier for you to practise than for many others, on account of your quiet, hidden life, very like that of the Holy Family at Nazareth. .... A great step must soon be taken—the sub-diaconate—a step for life and for eternity! Oh, pray for me, that I may in all things follow God's will, and that I may fully know what He requires of me. Say the 'Memorare' frequently for me with this intention. You know how I thank and love you beforehand for all you have already done for me in that and a thousand other ways."

To his father he writes,—

"I am now at an age when my future career must be decided upon, and perhaps there may be a question of my marriage. All this might have been a subject of great anxiety and trouble to you. But, my dearest father, I have chosen my own

path. Do not seek for an earthly partner for me.
Our Lord has called me, utterly unworthy as I am.
He has asked for my whole heart, for my body,
soul, and spirit, and can I refuse Him what is His?
And then I turn in thought to you, from whom,
next to God, I have received all—to you, my
darling father, and I ask, do not you wish the same
thing for me? Are you not willing to give me up
to God? *To give me up without reserve; to make
a complete sacrifice of your child?* Oh, I am sure
you will say yes! For if you have a father's
heart, you have equally the heart of a fervent,
loving Catholic. . . . . But I would add one
word more. Is it not the father who takes the
bride to the house of God? Who gives her to
her spouse? Do not her friends and relations
accompany her? Oh, I am sure you will do the
same by me! You will come to this my marriage,
the mysterious union which joins a human soul to
its Creator. You will come to offer to God the
child He has given you. You will come and bless
me not only in your own name, but in that of her
who I feel sure is now helping us with her prayers
before the Throne of God. You will bless me for
my mother."

We add to this touching letter the few words he
addressed to his godmother on the same occasion:—
"I hasten to tell you a piece of news. Perhaps
my dear godmother has forgotten that the little
child she carried to the Baptismal Font is now
twenty-one, the age required by the Church for
the office of sub-deacon. Well, I have made up
my mind, or rather it is not I that have settled it,
but God, who has chosen one so miserable and unworthy as I to serve at His altar. And can I say
'No'? I can only adore the mercy of God, and
nature must submit. So, on the 21st of this month

I am to be ordained sub-deacon. My father, I
trust, will come to the sacrifice of his son; but
I have no mother left on earth. Dare I ask my
godmother (my mother in the order of grace) to
take her place?"

The day of immolation came, and the sacrifice
was consummated. Then the young sub-deacon
sought his Director with the words, " Now I am
ready—you will no longer oppose my wish? you
will let me go?" And the good and prudent Director
assented, and at once wrote to obtain his admission
to the Foreign Missionary College. His much-
loved sister and little brother were unable to be
present at his ordination; but to console them he
wrote the following :—

"DEAREST MÉLANIE,—Your brother is at last
sub-deacon! My soul overflows with joy, but with
a joy so sweet and so pure that I cannot express
it. I should like to be able to tell you all I feel,
but I cannot put it into words. I took the terrible
step without trembling. God, in His infinite goodness, spared me the agony of fear at the moment.
My knees did not knock against each other, nor
did my foot fail me. When I was stretched on the
pavement I was only filled with a solemn calm;
but when I got up I felt as if I had broken every
link, as if I were for the first time free—free like
a little bird who has escaped from the snare of the
fowler. Oh, how willingly would I then have flown
up to heaven!"

To his brother he writes more gaily :—

"MY DEAR LITTLE EUSEBIUS,—Henry IV. said,
'Hang thyself, brave Crillon! we have won a
victory, and thou wert not there!' I shall say,
too, 'You were not there when your poor old

brother, prostrate on the pavement, gave himself irrevocably to God!' But I know well that it was not your fault, therefore please not to hang yourself! but help me to thank our dear Lord for the great grace He has bestowed upon me, and for the happiness with which I am filled. *Gratias Deo super inenarrabili dono ejus!* Oh, it was a grand day, and a day that has no ending—*quæ nescit occasum dies!* its dawn will be brighter and brighter until we come to eternity. And now, my dearest little brother, I feel as if I had acquired a right to say to you, 'Do not love the world or its pleasures.' They are all attractive and beautiful to our outward seeming; but within all is corruption, and vileness, and emptiness, and remorse. O my brother, let us love God, our dear, good God, and be as sheep under His hand! Love Him, and you will have no cause for repentance even on this earth. He, too, promises us joys and pleasures, but they are joys certain, inexpressible, eternal, —*pax Dei quæ exsuperat omnem sensum!*"

The answer soon came from Paris, and it was favourable. Then the young student began to make his preparations to leave the Poictiers Seminary, bid adieu to his family, and start joyfully for that house which for the last two centuries has trained Apostles for China and Tonquin.

CHAPTER III.

THÉOPHANE'S departure was definitively settled, and it became necessary to break the news to his family, and especially to his father, who, proud of his son, had already made endless schemes for his future advancement. Théophane knew this; and although he thoroughly appreciated his father's courage and generosity, he yet shrunk, as his favourite child, from inflicting a blow which, he well knew, would be the annihilation of all his hopes. Nevertheless, he could not bear that a strange hand should give the tidings, and so he summoned courage to pen the following letter, which we give in its entirety.

"*February* 7, 1851.

"My dearest Father,—It is a little more than a month ago that, to my great joy, you came to be a witness to my consecration to the service of God. You, yourself, as it were, presented the victim at the altar. A poor and miserable offering indeed! yet such as it was our Lord in His infinite mercy accepted it. And since that moment how the time has flown! God guides the hearts of men, and they follow as He leads. God, as it were, took me by the hand, and spoke to me with an irresistible voice, 'My son!' He said, 'come, follow Me, fear nothing; you are little, and poor, and weak, and miserable, but I am the Almighty God.' Come, I will be with thee!' and I, can I have a will in presence of the will of God?

"My dearly-loved father, have you understood me? One day God said to Abraham, 'Take thy only-begotten son, Isaac, whom thou lovest, and go into the land of Vision; and there thou shalt offer him for a holocaust upon one of the mountains which I shall show thee.' And Abraham obeyed without a moment's hesitation, and without a murmur; and his obedience was most pleasing to God. Now, my dearest father, do you begin to understand me? Here am I, the child whom you love; I have not borrowed a strange pen to tell you the truth. I come openly, without any subterfuges, unworthy of us both. God calls me; yes, it is His call. Oh, call me likewise; say that you, too, are willing that your Théophane should become a missionary!

"Poor father! the word is said,—the *Foreign Missions*. Do not let your human nature shrink from the thought. Rather kneel and take your crucifix, that crucifix which received my mother's last breath, and say, 'My God, I consent, may Thy holy will be done. Amen.'

"O my father, forgive me for having struck the blow myself! Some people will tell you I am mad, ungrateful, a bad son, and I know not what besides. My darling father, you will not think so! I know you have a great and generous soul, and one that has drunk deeply at the only true source of real strength and greatness—that of Religion and Faith. I have saddened your heart; my own is sorrowful and heavy too. The sacrifice asked of us is hard—most hard! But, O Lord Jesus! since Thou dost will it, I will will it likewise, and so will my father.

"Courage, then, my dearest father—courage, and resignation and confidence in God and in His Holy Mother. Let us pray for each other. Father, I kneel at your feet. Bless your child, and believe in his respectful devotion and dutiful submission.

"Théophane Vénard, Sub-deacon."

As he knew beforehand, this letter came upon his father as a thunder-clap; but nevertheless the blow did not leave a sting behind, for M. Vénard was a large-hearted and generous Catholic. His answer, which we subjoin, was one of consent, and a consent so heartily given that it rivalled the sublime virtue of his son. One day, when a friend was trying to console M. Vénard by assuring him that his son's vocation had been abundantly weighed and proved by his superiors before they gave their assent, he exclaimed, "And what would become of the prophecy of our Lord Jesus Christ, who declared that His Gospel should be preached throughout the whole earth, if directors of colleges and heads of families were to check the aspirations of all the young students who wish to embark in the foreign missions?"

Such was the frank, loyal, generous nature of the father of the future missionary, and his character is well shown in the following letter:—

"St. Loup, *February* 12, 1851.

"My dearest well-beloved Son,—I will not attempt to describe the emotion your letter caused me. I fancy you had calculated beforehand the force of the blow. You may well say that the sacrifice is hard. Your ordination cost me nothing. On the contrary, it fulfilled my fondest wishes for you, and I was quite content. But now every thing is changed. All my plans are upset. Well may people say, 'Man proposes, and God disposes.' I had flattered myself that you would some day have a Cure near me, that I should be able to make over every thing to Henry, and then come and finish my days quietly under your roof, so that you should close my eyes. Happy, but, alas! hopeless illusions.

"My child, I cannot attempt to try and turn you from your great and holy resolutions. Neither will I sadden your heart by reproaches. I will content myself with asking you if, at your age, you think you can really arrive at so serious a decision and not regret it hereafter? But if you are resolved, if you feel that God has indeed called you, then I would say, 'Obey Him without hesitation.' Let nothing keep you back. Not even the thought of the poor old father whom you leave in his sorrowful desolation, nor of the paternal roof which will no longer shelter you. Enough; I know that he who puts his hand to the plough must not look behind him; I know also that he who leaves father and mother to follow his Lord will receive an eternal recompense, and such reasons are unanswerable. . . . I could not reply to your letter at once, my dearest son, for poor human nature would have its way at first. But to-day I am a little calmer, and I hasten to fulfil your wishes. You ask for my consent. I give it you without restriction. My blessing—O my dearest boy, why should I refuse it to you? You know that I only belong to my children, and that you may always reckon on me. All that gives you pleasure gives it to me likewise, cost what it will. My sacrifices began when you first went to school, and I was separated from you; they went on increasing year by year, and now God knows where they are to end! Well, I can only resign myself, and leave all in the hands of God, who, perhaps, will give me back my Isaac, as you have compared me to the Father of the Faithful.

"Do not let my letter sadden you too much. I cannot put my ideas down as I wish, but you will guess my thoughts. Let us hope that God will sustain us both in this great trial. Although your sister knew of your intention beforehand, she was terribly affected by your declaration, for she flattered herself the time was still far off. But, as you say, the time is short. . . . Henry saw at once that there was something the matter, but I

have told him nothing as yet. And poor little
Eusebius, whom you were to mould and form, is he
to lose his model and his guide? Forgive my saying this—forgive your poor old father, who lives
but in his children. I feel I have gone too far,
and that I shall give you pain, and you don't
deserve it.

"Bear in mind, then, that I freely give my consent to your plans. Be at peace, and do not trouble
about me. The hand of God is every where. I
love you with all my heart, and embrace you
tenderly. "VÉNARD."

So the future missionary could go to the Foreign
Missionary College without fear, and instead of the
anger of his father, he was to meet with nothing
but love and blessings. Théophane's feelings found
vent in the following letter to his sister :—

"MY DARLING SISTER,—Oh, how I cried when I
read your letter! Yes, I know well the sorrow I was
going to bring upon my family, and especially upon
you, my dear little sister. But don't you think it
cost me tears of blood, too, to take such a step, and
give you all such pain? Who ever cared more for
home and a home life than I? All my happiness
here below was centred in it. But God, who had
united us all in links of the tenderest affection,
wished to wean me from it. Oh, what a fight and a
struggle I have had with my poor human nature!
But then our Lord, who asked the sacrifice at my
hands, gave me the strength to accomplish it. He
did more. He gave me the courage to offer myself
the bitter chalice to those I loved. I undertook it
because I know you all so well, and I was full of
faith and hope; and that hope has not been disappointed. And now I can only adore His mercy,

and praise Him who has led me so tenderly through this terrible trial.

"Can it be, then, that family ties and family joys are not holy and blessed? Has God forbidden them? Or were our hearts too absorbed in them, so that God, to punish us, wished to withdraw them altogether? Or are we all gone crazy? No! no! a thousand times no! Let the world say what it will. What matters it to us, Children of Grace, who have received the heavenly promises? The world and its maxims have long ago received their condemnation from the mouth of our Divine Lord Himself. Ah! Lord God, Thy thoughts are not as our thoughts, and Thou walkest by paths of which the world knows nothing.

"See, my dearest sister, how He has led us until now. We had a good and darling mother, and she was taken from us just as we were entering upon life. How we have cried for her! But God took pity on her children. He has given you strength and wisdom to take her place in the family, and especially after our grandmother's death, who went softly from this life to one which was eternal, inviting us all to follow her. Then another sacrifice was asked of us. You, my good little sister, had long given yourself to God. You wanted to do so altogether, but Providence contented itself with your will and your submission, and did not exact the consummation of the sacrifice. But God was watching over your poor brother. He was conducting him as by the hand in a path traced out by Himself. Oh, miracle of Grace! Oh the depth and the riches of the goodness and mercy of God! He Who needs not human instruments to accomplish His great designs, chooses the vilest, the most miserable of His creatures to do His work. I, wretched little I, receive the mission and the inspiration of the Apostolate. . . . . Dearest sister, say with me our God is good—infinitely good. Let all the earth echo the words, and repeat them in a transport of gratitude and joy. See how our Lord loves us. See how He showers His gifts upon us. One more sacrifice is asked of us; but does not our Lord prove those He loves so as to make them more worthy of Himself? Must we not all pass through the crucible? A cross is given to us. Let us embrace it generously, and thank Him. Our tears must flow. Well, but let us offer them up to Him who has called them forth. This earth is after all but a valley of tears; and the Divine Master has said, 'Blessed are those that mourn, for they shall be comforted.' And then, even if we do part here for a little time, it is only our bodies that are separated. Our souls are united more closely than ever in thoughts which know no space or distance. We shall meet one another in heaven. Oh yes, all of us shall be together then. Let us trust in God, and make the sacrifice generously. And then you have Henry; and God will watch over poor little Eusebius. Let us pray and trust and hope, and remain united to each other in the hearts of Jesus and Mary. . . And now I must add a line to my dear father. Oh, you don't know how proud I am to be his son! I long to feel myself in his arms, pressed to his heart. . . . . My father, with your grand courage, firm faith, burning love—all for God—even your Théophane! Dearest father, these souls that I am going to strive and win for our Lord I offer them all to you, next to God. They will be your crown and your glory in the Home of the Elect.

"I am going away, but I leave you an angel of consolation—a loving guardian angel—in Mélanie. When the time of your pilgrimage is over, Mélanie will close your eyes, will pray by your bedside, and

will speak to you of your poor little missionary;
and you will bless her and him too. But why do
I speak of death? Oh, please God, you will live
many, many years yet to be the joy and the providence of your children! The little missionary will
get letters from you from time to time, and news of
all the family, and that will be a great joy to him. I
hope also to spend a *good long fortnight* with my dear
belongings, and enjoy them thoroughly before I start."

The "little missionary" accordingly came home
on Saturday, the 15th February. He arranged to
come on foot from Parthenay, so as to meet his
brother Henry, and have a talk with him before
they saw their father. The only idea of there
being something extraordinary going to happen
was from a little note Théophane had written to
both his brothers in these words: "I implore you to
say the 'Memorare' for me every day till we meet,
so that I may obtain a great grace. You will soon
know why." But the poor children were far from
guessing the truth.

Henry being then eighteen, at once understood
the gravity and importance of the step which his
brother was about to take. As for poor little
Eusebius, his uncertainty came to an end on the
morrow, when Théophane came to carry him off for
a fortnight from his studies. He had set his heart
on having his whole family together on this occasion, and to enjoy for the last time the happiness
which such a home circle alone can give.

It is easy to understand how trying these last
few days were to them all; but to Théophane it
was the hardest of all. He had to be tender,
affectionate, and loving to every one, and yet firm
and determined in his resolution to leave them. At
times he could scarcely contain himself, and had to

do incessant violence to his own heart to maintain
any kind of decent calmness. But, on the whole,
he acquitted himself marvellously.

We cannot attempt to describe his first meeting
with his father. They embraced each other closely
in silence, without tears or sighs. Only after a
time the words, "My dearest boy!" "My good
father!" burst from the lips of each. But these few
words said all to those who could feel and understand what was passing in those two loving hearts.

These touching scenes were renewed very often
in the course of this trying fortnight, especially
towards evening, when they drew near the fireside after dinner, when there would often be a
dead silence, the father contenting himself with
pressing his son's hand, not daring to trust himself
to speak. But then the future missionary would
try and cheer them all by droll stories, or interest
them in the countries he was so soon about to visit.
At last he excited them so on the subject of China
and the missions, that nothing would content Mélanie and his brothers but the thought of going
too. They made a thousand little plans, in which
each was to share in his labours. "And what is
to become of me?" at last exclaimed their father,
who had been silently listening to their fine projects; "am I to be left like poor old Zebedee to
mend my nets? Rather than that I will go too."
Indeed, he several times told his son that nothing
but his duty to his other children kept him back,
adding that he had nothing any longer to bind
him to life; and that all he asked of God was to
be allowed time to launch his children in life, and
then sing his "Nunc Dimittis."

And so the days sped on, only too rapidly, and
each evening became more sad as each grew nearer
and nearer to the one which was to hear the last

farewell. Poor Mélanie felt it especially, and every night would linger after the others, to get the last kiss and the last word. There was always something more to say, and the last night of all they did not attempt to go to bed. Mélanie had several little things to add to his outfit; and he sat watching her, and saying as many loving things as his sad heart would allow. Ten years after, Théophane, then a Confessor for the Faith, remembered every single incident of that night, which consoled him even in the bottom of his cage. Only two days before his final martyrdom, he wrote to his sister, "It was alone with you that I passed that delicious night of the 26th February, 1851; that night at home which was the scene of our last interview on earth, spent in holy, helpful, consoling talk like that of St. Benedict and his sister."

The day of departure came at last. The whole family sought strength where alone it could be found, and received the Holy Communion together. Théophane himself served the Mass with a rapt manner and expression, which made him look more like an angel than a man. Then came farewell visits to friends and relations, when he tried to turn aside sorrowful thoughts and anticipations by a bright, gay manner, and little jokes now and then; yet he owned afterwards that he was nearly suffocated with sorrow. One visit only cost him many tears, it was to the churchyard, and the tomb of his mother, that mother whom he had so idolized, and from whom he had been separated at the hour of her death, so that he had never had her dying blessing—to him a cause of eternal regret. He could scarcely tear himself away from those precious remains. And yet the thought of this visit was most consoling to him afterwards, and he always spoke of it with tears of gratitude.

The hour of departure had been fixed for nine o'clock in the evening. Théophane had chosen that time, to avoid a crowd of anxious and sympathizing friends; his brother and one old friend were to drive him to Parthenay, where he was to take the night train. They sat down to dinner rather earlier than usual, the good old pastor of the village having joined them; and Théophane, by almost superhuman efforts, succeeded in making the meal cheerful, and almost gay. But a few words from his father towards the end brought back sad and sorrowful thoughts, and they all got more and more silent. The dinner was over, and the time of departure was drawing nearer every moment. As usual they said the Rosary together, and then read a chapter of the Imitation, after which they knelt for Evening Prayers. But no one had the courage to lead them save Théophane himself, and as he went on, the sobs and tears of his little audience became the more audible. It is so true, that whatever restraint we may put upon our feelings before men, the barrier breaks down when we find ourselves alone with God! Théophane with difficulty finished the prayer, and rose, and then approaching his father said, "The hour is come; we must part. My father, will you not bless your son, your poor little Théophane?" and he threw himself at his father's feet, embracing his knees. The poor father lifted his eyes and his hands to Heaven, and with a broken voice, making the sign of the Cross on his child's head, said, "My dearest son, receive the blessing of your father, who offers you a willing sacrifice to our Lord. May you be blessed for ever and for ever, in the name of the Father, and of the Son, and of the Holy Ghost. Amen!"

Then Théophane rising, knelt for a moment in

the same way for the good old priest's blessing, and then rapidly kissed his whole family, as he did each evening before going to bed ; but this was for the last time ! Henry went out to see if the carriage was ready. Eusebius threw himself into his brother's arms, sobbing as if his little heart would break. Mélanie, kissing him and crying " Only once more," fell back almost fainting on her chair. The poor father, still and immovable from excess of sorrow, lent heavily on the arm of his old friend the Curé.

" Courage ! let us be generous in our sacrifices !" murmured the poor missionary. He could bear no more. With one last kiss to his half-unconscious sister, he seized his cloak and hat, and rushed into the carriage. Then several friends and townspeople crowded round him, to shake hands for the last time. He wrung their hands, exclaiming, " Good-bye ! good-bye ! we shall meet in our true home," and the carriage set off rapidly for Parthenay. The sacrifice was over, and M. Vénard without wronging his other children could say, " I have lost the fairest flower in my garden !" The delay at the moment of departure, though slight, made them miss the train at Parthenay by five minutes. This was a minor but very real trial to our poor Théophane, who longed for the final parting to be over. But there was no help for it, and so they waited for the next train, which started at six o'clock in the morning. His brother remarked that when once settled in the railway carriage, Théophane looked away, and then, burying his face in his hands, he cried bitterly and uncontrollably to relieve the poor heart which had had such difficulty in containing itself during the last twenty-four hours.

CHAPTER IV.

THREE days after the sad parting we have just recorded, Théophane left Poictiers for Paris, and arrived at the Foreign Missionary College. There the same hearty welcome met him that we have already described in the Life of Henry Dorié. "Hardly had I come into the house," he wrote to his sister, "but that I was met with affectionate greetings on all sides, and every sort of kindness was showered upon me. One hoisted up my trunk into my cell; another uncorded it; a third made my bed and showed me where my little establishment was to be; a fourth took me all over the house, introduced me to the Directors, and showed me the garden. In half an hour I felt as if I knew them all intimately. Oh the good their welcome did to my poor sad heart! There is nothing like the love and charity of this house, and the way they make one feel at home at once."

As the little series of missionary lives which we are writing is specially meant for the new College now being started in the neighbourhood of London, may we venture to draw the attention of the students very particularly to this feature in the French seminary? We do not imagine that hearts beat less warmly one side of the Channel than the other. But we cannot help regretting the coldness which seems inseparable from most Englishmen in their dealings with each other, and which sends a chill through hearts who have just gone through the wrench of parting with all they hold most dear. Surely it would be more in accordance with the spirit of our Great Master if we were to go out of our way to show little unselfish kindnesses, and a little more of the true Christian courtesy which distinguishes our French and Italian brethren.

This spirit of charity and mutual kindness is the distinguishing characteristic of the Foreign Missionary College in Paris. Its Divine fire is carefully maintained by its superiors as the best means of spreading its genial rays to the extremities of the heathen world. In the midst of a great city, and a world gone drunk with dissipation and business of all sorts, these young men find there an abode of peace and quietness indeed, but no ascetic solitude. Rather is it a home where each strives who shall be foremost in loving, kindly ways, and consideration for the other; and the Holy Spirit seems specially to bless this atmosphere of mutual charity and forbearance, and to pour His sevenfold gifts on the future Apostles, who are learning in that best of schools (for it is our Lord's), the school of love.

Théophane was thoroughly happy here, although it did not altogether do away with the bitterness of separation from those he held most dear.

He writes, "We are all like one family here, with one object and one aim. We have no care or troubles, and I should have nothing left to wish for if you were by my side. I am greatly touched by your anxiety about me, my dearest father; but you must let me scold you about this a little bit. Am I not more than ever the child of Providence? Did you not yourself give me up to Him? He who watches over the birds of the air, and the flowers of the field, will He not take care of me wherever I may be? I cannot help longing for you, and missing you terribly sometimes; but love suffers and is resigned, and the thoughts of Heaven grow more vivid as we get more detached from all on earth. Only a little more trust! A little more confidence in God! A little more patience! and then the end will come, and the past weary years will seem as nothing; and then will arrive the moment of reunion, and all will be amply compensated for and repaid, principal and interest. O Christian hope! How beautiful thou art! How thou dost satisfy the heart of man, the creature of a day, and yet created for an eternity of bliss!"

His family could not at once rise to his level of superhuman caring, and their letters were full of the void he had left behind, and their despair at losing him. All his answers, therefore, were written at this time with a view to heal the wound he had caused, and he had always a kind and loving word for the consolation of each. To Henry he writes, "Your letter touched me very much, and especially where you say that the thought of me is not enough—that you want my *bodily* presence to comfort you. I feel just the same about you all. My thoughts fly home to the little room where you all are in the evening, and to my place by Mélanie's side, and to the thousand and one recollections of our boyhood. But it is God's Will that we should be separated. May that Will be for ever blessed; and after all, are we not bound for the same haven? Will not the gaps in the family circle then be filled up? Nay, more, are we not already waited for *up there* by one most near and dear to us? You recollect our last visit before leaving home—a visit paid at your suggestion—that visit to the cemetery, where we prayed and cried so together for our darling mother? Well, very soon we shall go and join her; and the links that bind us are tightened at the thought, and the time which seems so long and weary is bridged over."

To his sister he says, "If I have read your dear letter over once, I have read it twenty times!

Every word you say goes to my heart, for we are one, are we not? with the same feelings, the same tastes, the same wishes, the same hopes. We really are, as the saying is, born for each other; and how comes it, then, that we are separated? Why, because God wished that we should be united eternally. As you said yourself one day, dearest Mélanie, if we could live together here below, we should have cared too much for the world, and so He has divided us that our souls should be more and more purified, and sigh more and more after the moment when they shall take their flight to Heaven. A great servant of God once said, 'That if some gall were not mingled in our earthly cup, we should be content with our exile, and think less of our own true country.' .. "

To his little brother he sends also a word of loving sympathy: "You cannot imagine the pleasure your letters have given me. I know well my poor little brother's tender, loving heart, but I rejoice that you have struggled against your sorrow, and not given way to it too much. You have thrown yourself into Mary's arms as a child into the arms of its mother. What a comfort it is to be able to do that in our moments of loneliness and desolation. Let Mary always be your refuge, my darling brother! The Blessed Virgin is much loved and honoured in the College here. When you have any little sorrow or trouble, then go simply to her, and ask her to offer it up for you to our dear Lord, and there leave it, without any further care or preoccupation. Then you will have nothing to fear either from men or devils. You will walk quietly in the path of life until you come hopefully to that home where we all sigh and wish to be!"

After what we have told our readers, it is not to

be wondered at that Théophane not only won all
hearts at the College, but made rapid progress in
the paths of perfection. His humility and simplicity concealed even from himself the beauty of
his soul, but it could not be hidden from his
superiors, or still less from his holy and wise
director. Among the students, two of them,
M. Dallet and M. Theurel, soon won a high
place in his affections. But fearful lest the tie
should become too human, they mutually agreed to
tell each other their faults, and so to make their
very intimacy a means of advancing more rapidly
in their heaven-bound path. Théophane fulfilled
this compact conscientiously, and it might have
been thought almost severely, if his words had
not been tempered by such extreme humility and
sweetness that it disarmed all inclination to
wounded feeling. As far as he himself was
concerned, he was his own severest accuser, and
often his humility led him to exaggerate his
shortcomings to such an extent that he honestly
believed himself utterly unfit for the apostolic
life he had chosen, and besought the prayers of
all his friends for his conversion. He even had
himself publicly recommended at Notre Dame des
Victoires, and, writing to a lady who had been
preparing various little things for his future
chapel, he says, "I am not sure of being allowed
to go. I feel myself so utterly unworthy! Not
that my desire is altered: on the contrary, I am
more firmly resolved than ever. But the decision
does not rest with me. May His holy will be
done! But after all, if they think me unworthy
of the missionary life, you must not be troubled;
for it is not for me you have been working, but
for God; and if I do not make use of your gifts,
you will find no difficulty in placing them else-

where. And indeed, if I thought you were working for me, I should be in great distress to know how to repay you for your kindness and zeal. But, thank God, I know that it is for Him you labour—to Him that you have devoted your life. He reserves for you a glorious crown, and the brightest flower in that crown will be your co-operation in this work of the Foreign Missions. Oh, what a joy would it be to me at that great day, when the prizes will be distributed by the hand of unerring justice, if I might hear your name and your merit recognized and rewarded, and be permitted to sing 'Amen' to the solemn declaration which will admit you into the land of everlasting light and love—into the presence of our dear Lord and Saviour Jesus Christ, and of His holy Mother, and of all His holy angels and saints!"

Théophane was ordained Deacon at Christmas in 1851, and wrote with delight of the Retreat which was to precede his ordination.

"On Sunday evening next we go into Retreat till the Saturday following, a holy and happy time of meditation and prayer, dwelling under the shadow of the altar, free from cares and distractions, absorbed in God. Fancy a delicious day in spring, with a pure sky, all nature bursting forth into leaf and blossom, or the deep calm of a tomb. . . . Ah, it is better than all this, for it is Heaven begun on earth, God communicating Himself to man, man raising and uniting himself to God! Ah, dear friend, what happiness He allows to His creatures!"

Then came the ordination. He writes, "The ordination was very large, and all the different communities of Paris contributed some members. I found, kneeling side by side with me, Lazarists, Dominicans, Franciscans, Missionaries of the Holy Ghost, Irish, Negroes, &c. I knew none of them;

but my heart went out to them with love and
sympathy, for are we not children of the same
Father, servants of the same Master, soldiers of the
same King. The same object unites us; the same
grace, in different degrees, was distributed to us;
the same God gave Himself to us; and we invoked the same Queen, Mary, the Mother of the
Saviour of the world. And then, as brothers, we
gave one another the kiss of Peace. Oh, how
happy I was!"

Théophane had a special devotion to Church
music, and especially to the old hymns and can-
ticles of the Church. He wrote of them as
follows:—

"The hymns of the Church have always had a
peculiar charm for me, and the more I hear them
the more I long to hear, and the oftener I sing them
the oftener I like to sing, for it is the voice of man
in his exile, and the voice of the Church, praying,
hoping, loving. Would that my countrymen would
go back to the good old days of a purer and
stronger faith, and not be ashamed to sing together
the songs of their forefathers! Now they only
care for political or revolutionary ditties; a
malediction on those who have swept away the
faith and the hope of our people, who have robbed
them of their peace and their tranquillity! France
used to be so calm and happy. But, no; we will
curse no one. Only, may God have mercy on us
all!"

But Théophane was not to see only the inside of
the Seminary. He was sent on several occasions
into the great world of Paris, and of this wonderful capital he writes thus to his brother Henry:—

"At Paris we are in the midst of two extremes
of vice and virtue—vice of the lowest and most
degrading kind, and virtue the most heroic! In

returning from Meudon, which is our little country house, about two leagues from Paris, I constantly pass through the Bois de Boulogne. It is a magnificent park, beautifully laid out with walks and drives, shaded by fine trees, and full of beautiful flowers. It is crowded with people on foot, in carriages, and on horseback. On leaving the park you pass through the Barrière de l'Étoile, and its triumphal arch, to an avenue which leads to the Place de la Concorde. This avenue is planted with trees, and on either side you see fine houses and beautiful villas. There is even a greater crowd here than in the Bois. The greater portion are pleasure-hunters. Do they find it? Well, perhaps those do who care for nothing but dissipation and jollity. But happiness? No; happiness is to be found only in home and in the domestic circle, where God is loved and honoured, and every one loves, and helps, and cares for the other. The great cry now is, 'the People.' The word written up every where is (Fraternité) 'Brotherhood.' In Paris they have well-nigh abolished the idea of Family Life. If I were not afraid of vexing some really good souls among them, I should say that Paris was nothing but a scene of confusion, a heterogeneous mass, where no one knew or cared for or respected the other. To realize the true meaning of Brotherhood it should be written not on the walls, but in the heart. There is a beautiful reciprocity of feeling in the different relations of life, where all are united in the one great love in Him who gave His life for us, our Lord and Saviour Jesus Christ! If only every one could feel this, how perfect would be the harmony on earth!" . .

To Eusebius he writes,—"You want me to describe Paris to you? Well, let us get out at the Orleans Railway Station, where the rail ends from

Poictiers, and we shall find ourselves on the Quays
which line the Seine, or rather which restrict it
within very narrow bounds, and into which all the
drains are emptied, so that the water is any thing
but sweet and clear like our Thouet. . . . The
Tuileries gardens would be the next object of
interest to you, and I should praise them like the
Luxembourg if it were not so peopled with Pagan
deities! Now you are in the very heart of the
Parisian world. You see beautiful mansions, brilliant
equipages, elegant dandies, beautiful ladies
strutting like peacocks, but who, it seems to me,
want to go to school again to learn modesty,
humility, and even common sense. Every body
lounges about, either here or in the museums, or
in the galleries of the Palais Royal, or in the Jardin
des Plantes, or in the Bois de Boulogne, where the
only object seems to be to see and be seen. Here
are a whole tribe of nurses with their babies; and
the monkeys are showing off their tricks, and the
fountains are playing, and the jugglers are trying
to make people laugh. . . . Well, have not these
people really earned their dinners? Then comes
the evening, when every one seems to think it
necessary to go to some theatre or other, or to
some ball, winding up with ice and coffee in the
Boulevards, if not in their drawing-rooms; and the
gas lights up the city all night, and the world goes
to bed when the sun is rising. What a day for a
reasonable being, let alone a Christian! This
is Paris life, the life of people in the world who
fancy they have found happiness. Frankly, the
whole thing disgusts and wearies me to death. I
should never end if I were to tell you how ridiculous
poor human nature appears in a thousand ways
when left to itself, regardless of God, our good
God, the only end and aim of life! One gives

himself the airs of a philosopher, another, of a poet;
this one has a passion for music, that one for
pictures. Every one talks politics, of which
three-parts know nothing whatever. It is really
humiliating to hear them! Oh, you cannot think,
after I have been elbowed half a day by all these
worldly people, what a relief it is to me to come
back to the College! How I love its cool, quiet
cloisters, the peace in its cells, the hours of study
and meditation, the gaiety of its recreations, the
charity and good-will of its inmates, the charm of
its chapel, the recollection of its history, the indescribable 'something' which seems to speak to us
all day of the Apostolate and martyrdom! ... One
day I went to Versailles; I saw its enormous
castle, and gardens, and park, but I could not feel
enthusiastic about any of them. I kept on thinking, 'Well, after all, this is all that man can
produce of magnificence and splendour. How
miserably unsatisfactory!' Ah, but all earthly
things fade so before the thoughts of Heaven!...
You ask me about the sights, the inventions, and
the balloons. Well, as to the latter, the ladies
themselves are the most marvellous specimens!
Even in heathen times, I verily believe such things
would have been scouted. If man would give the
glory of his inventions to God, they might bring a
blessing; but we see nothing, hear of nothing, but
materialism and "nature." God help both France
and Europe! ... If you ever come here you will
be as struck as I am at the marvellous dissipation
of this place, the never-ending turmoil, and bustle,
and noise, and unrest. Oh, how I hate these never-
ending streets, which tire my feet, my eyes, and my
ears, where the world and its views reign supreme,
and the one object of every living being seems to
be pleasure, and pleasure only! In the midst of

this impious city real saints are found, but most of those who have eyes do not see them or know them. They are hidden from the crowd and known but to God, and, thank Him, they are multiplying. Oh, Christianity is not dead, as the gentlemen of the Voltaire school are pleased to say!" .... After dwelling a little longer on Paris and its sights, he exclaims, "But what is the use of my going on talking to you of all these vanities and follies. I went the other day to Notre Dame to see all the splendid decorations which were used on New Year's Day, 1852, when Louis Napoleon made his triumphal entry into the cathedral. Well, what struck me most of all was the thought of how the great ones of the earth were thus compelled to do homage to the majesty of God and to the glory of His Church. God alone is the sovereign beauty, and His works perfect and glorious. If man be ever so great, it is only when he draws his inspirations from God, and when, in heartfelt humility, he gives to Him the glory. In Catholic countries all human potentates seek the support of the Church, for she is the one power—first and indestructible—and without her aid no Catholic government can exist, for the winds and the tempests would blow and sweep it away from off the face of the earth."

This, surely, is a grand view to take of the political situation of a great Catholic country. In 1848 Théophane had been painfully moved by the debate in the National Assembly; and when he came to Paris he asked and obtained permission to go to the Chambers and hear the principal speakers. He gave an account of his impressions to his father, and his sinister previsions were soon realized. The political horizon became more and more darkened, and the agitation was at its height, when the

Coup d'État of the 2nd of December gave the signal for a fresh revolution. On this event Théophane wrote as follows:—"My dearest Father,—It is ten o'clock in the morning. Paris is declared in a state of siege. The National Assembly is dissolved." . . . Then he goes on to relate facts well known to our readers, and subjoins, "May our good God come to our aid, and direct all to His honour and glory! Let us pray for France and for all Europe. We have been expecting this shock from day to day, and so we are not troubled. When and how will it all end? Human events succeed one another so rapidly, and then pass away. God alone is immutable—let us go to Him! After all, what does the future matter to us? If the world were destroyed, we should be safe in Him and in the bosom of His Church. The works of men alone remain—let them, then, be works of charity and justice. All this seems to me to detach one more and more from things of earth, and to fix one's thoughts and heart on Heaven." To another college friend he writes, "To remedy the evil, France must be converted, or else God will permit the working classes, the men who possess nothing, to be sooner or later the instruments of His vengeance. It seems to me our business is to try and become each one of us better, and then God will have pity upon our country. . . As far as I am concerned, I assure you I am in perfect safety. Our congregation is looked upon with a favourable eye at Paris, and every one knows and is kind to us. In February, 1848, the eve of the dethronement of Louis Philippe, our community was going across the Champs Elysées. An immense crowd was collected, and some of them deliberated what they should do to them. But the majority exclaimed, 'Let us leave them alone. Those are the men who are going to *martyrize* themselves in China!' and the observation saved our poor missionaries.

"The 4th of December we remained almost all day near the Bois de Boulogne. A detachment of cuirassiers were galloping toward Paris, where the fighting had begun. The workmen were in the streets, quiet and orderly, but anxious. They were very civil to us. The next day three of our students were obliged to go through the streets where they had already erected barricades. The soldiers were bivouacking by their fires, a dense mob thronged round them, sullen and silent, and breathing nothing but vengeance; but they allowed our missionaries to pass without molestation, and even showed them marks of kindness and good will."

After the *Coup d'État*, the agitation ceased, and people gradually became calmer. Théophane wrote hopefully to his godmother: "The new government seems well disposed towards religion, and willing to give the Church her due. If they go on so, God will send His blessing on this poor distracted country, and there may be some chance of seeing things reorganized. Since our Lord Jesus Christ became man, His Divine manhood must take the lead in human affairs; for a people calling itself Christian, and throwing off all allegiance to the Most High, becomes thoroughly ungovernable, for the simple reason that corruption is greater when it shows itself in what was originally good. Those who think they can see farther than their neighbours are hopeful as to the future of France, which makes me sanguine too. Although I may soon be far away, I shall always look anxiously for tidings of my country's welfare. May God bring about a brighter day! Amen." He ends with the beautiful words,—

"O my Lord, Thy people know and love Thee by instinct; but they are deceived by their chiefs, who betray and mislead them. Oh, if only all the world were of one heart and one mind to serve and honour and glorify Thee!"

At the risk of wearying our readers, we are tempted to give one or two more extracts from our holy missionary's letters to his family during the remainder of his stay at the Foreign Missionary College; for these letters are so full of wise and holy counsel, especially those to his youngest brother, that we have felt that they might be of equal value to others in a like position.

Eusebius had just entered "Le Petit Séminaire;" he was fifteen, and with a strong desire to become a priest. Under these circumstances he writes to Théophane for advice; and the elder brother answers as follows:—

"MY DEAR EUSEBIUS,—You are now of an age to choose your future career; an age when people begin to think, and when certain convictions form themselves in our minds and influence our conduct. In your intercourse with men, you will encounter much prejudice, many strange ideas, and perversions of the truth; for their minds have wandered from the good old paths; and society in Europe has become thoroughly corrupt. I do not mean to say that there were not plenty of bad people in old times, as there are now, for man is ever the same. But formerly there were certain social bases and landmarks which none but the very vicious overpassed. For religion was the foundation of society, and God gives life to nations as well as to individuals. Now all these safeguards are removed or ignored, but you will understand this better by and by.

"Well, you are asking yourself, what is to be your future? Pray, simply, humbly, and fervently, to know God's will, and your path will be made clear. Then you will follow the inspiration which Divine mercy has put into your heart. Some people say, 'I will be a priest,' or 'a soldier,' or 'a landed proprietor,' and then they add, 'Oh, such and such studies are not necessary for this or that profession!' This is the reasoning of pure idlers. Then others go on about piety: 'Piety! it is only good for priests and nuns. God does not expect so much of us!' (*How do you know?*) These are the arguments of cold and calculating natures. Now what I want you to say to yourself is, 'I am, first of all, a man, a reasonable being, created to know, love, serve, and glorify God. I come from God. I go to God. I belong to God. My body is His. My mind is His. My heart is His. I shall be judged according to my works, and to the way I have corresponded to the grace given me. Well then, God helping me, I will use this body, this mind, and this heart, as much as I possibly can for His greater glory, honour, and love.'

"My dear Eusebius, life well employed consists in this: *A faithful correspondence to grace, and a good use of the talents given.* There is no other religion than this, and the rule of life is the same for all.

"But you ask, 'What does God ask of *me?*' Humility, prayer, obedience to His Divine commands, and to the voice of our mother the Church, and an entire abandonment of ourselves to His Divine providence. You answer,—

"'But many men do not reason like this.'

"To God alone it pertaineth to judge of others. We have only to look to ourselves. For the mo-

ment, what you have to do is study with all your
might, to make use of the advantages which God
has put in your way, and which you owe, under
Him, to the generous love of our dear father.
Work, not to gain honour and distinction, but to
please God. He who does not work for God
works for the devil and for his friend, the world.
God is represented on earth by His Holy Catholic,
Roman, and Apostolic Church. She is the City
of God, whose citizens we are, no matter in what
corner of the earth our lot may be cast. Our Lord
Jesus Christ is the chief of this city; but we shall
not see this clearly until the consummation of all
things. The Pope and the Bishops are His representatives on earth, and have a permanent and
infallible authority to which we must submit, and
in which we must believe, as in Jesus Christ Himself. He who is not with them is against them.
The Catholic Church on earth is termed *Militant*
—that is, she is perpetually at war with Satan
and the world. Ever since her birth she has been
attacked on every side. Your business must be to
fight for her, and under her banner, taking the
saints as your protectors and guides. . . . . Do
not let yourself give way to vexation at little
troubles and cares. Banish the idea that such
and such things *bore* you. We have to learn very
early to live amidst constant contradictions and
mortifications of our natural tastes and inclinations. But it is this which trains us and makes
us good Soldiers of the Cross, and the soul is
thereby raised and purified. It is a trite saying
enough that there is no heaven without a cloud, and
that you mustn't expect any thing to be perfect in
this life, but what I want you to do is to bear
every thing cheerfully and gaily, to rejoice even
in vexatious; and if you can't be bright naturally,

to strive and be bright in and for God. . . . .
Try and be agreeable in conversation, good-
humoured and merry, and full of cheerfulness and
fun, not brooding on disagreeables. And now you
will say I have preached enough, and so I will
only add, having laid down certain great principles
for your life, forward! Don't be afraid of being
laughed at. You will crown all by keeping up the
tender love of a little child for the Blessed Virgin,
and a confiding trust in your Guardian Angel."

A little later he writes to him on his vocation.
" You tell me that your wishes, your tastes, a
secret inspiration of grace, draw you strongly
towards the priesthood. May God's Holy Name
be praised! but if our Lord calls you you must
answer. One day little Samuel heard a voice
crying out, 'Samuel, Samuel!' 'Here I am,
Lord,' he replied. *Ecce ego, Domine, quia vocasti
me.* Eusebius! you think our Lord has called
you. Well, then, you must answer like Samuel,
'"Here I am, Lord," what wilt Thou have me
to do? With the help of Thy grace I will do all
that Thou dost appoint, and that grace I feel will
not be wanting.'

"It is, then, on the 1st of October (that month
dedicated to the angels) that you are to leave
your country and your home, and your beautiful
valley, and go into a strange place. Courage!
When one leaves any thing for God He rewards us
a hundredfold; He has said so Himself. But
(you say) you are 'alone,' 'quite alone.' Oh,
no, you are the child of our Divine Lord and His
Blessed Mother, the child of His Love, the sheep
of His pasture; have confidence in God. Nevertheless, if there are times when your heart sinks
within you, go, my dearest brother, go to the

chapel, offer to our dear Lord your tears and your sacrifice, and then, alone before God, consecrate yourself anew without reserve to His service. Offer him, to begin with, the trials of your college life; throw yourself like a boy into the arms of Mary, and believe me when I say you will never be forsaken.

"You will have to choose a confessor, and for this you must pray earnestly to our Lord and His Mother to enlighten and guide you. Then, when you have chosen one, you must open your whole heart to him, not only in the confessional, but when you see him alone elsewhere; make him your friend and counsellor in all your little difficulties and sorrows, and tell him of your temptations and faults with thorough simplicity and openness. Then be guided by his advice, and follow it to the letter. This is the kind of spiritual direction necessary to one who seeks to advance towards perfection. Confide in him entirely, and be sure that he will keep all your little secrets as if it were in the confessional. You are no longer a child, dear Eusebius, and you must begin to walk as one worthy of the mercies of God, and of His great designs on your behalf. Make a little book in which you can write down your impressions, and your religious feelings now and then, putting the date; you can dedicate it to our Lady. Some day later you will read them over again with pleasure, and they will serve to brace you up when days of heaviness and weariness overcome your courage."

(Théophane had himself this practice, but, unfortunately, when he was ill, he insisted on burning all he had written.)

"Be very humble towards God, remembering your misery; and before men, in imitation of our Divine Master, who prepared Himself for

His public ministry by thirty years of a hidden and humble life. If you are really humble you will be charitable to your fellow-students, not seeking your own interest, but theirs, and devoting yourself to them, body and soul, even to those who occasionally give you pain or annoyance. I should like to think that you deprived yourself now and then of some indulgence to give to the poor. You ought not to run into great expenses, or attempt to imitate the luxurious habits of many of those around you. Remember your own simple home, and still more remember how many thousands there are who suffer the want of the very necessaries of life. Above all, never forget that God is in every thing; in little things as in great. He ought to be the one motive of your thoughts, words, and actions. Go often to confession, have great devotion to the Blessed Sacrament, and associate yourself as soon as you can with some congregation of our Lady. Oh, how happy I was when I first became a child of Mary! Go, then, dearest brother, and may the Angel of God guide your steps! A great future is before you; a grand vocation! Think of it well, and anchored on the infinite mercy of God, repeat humbly yet trustfully the saying of St. Paul, *Ad destinatum persequor, ad bravium supernæ vocationis in Christo Jesu!* . . . Oh, Eusebius, you are at the grandest moment of your life! Do you know why? Because it is in the age of strong passions, of great struggles, of great victories. Our Lord 'looks' upon a young man, and 'loves him;' that young man is yourself. Courage, then! be worthy of your Master. After the struggle what a reward! Perhaps you will hear a voice saying, "Come with me," and that we shall find ourselves soldiers of the same regiment, travellers on the same road, bound for the same haven. May His

Holy Will be done, and not ours. Leave your future in His hands—in the heart of Jesus made man. Recollect that He too was "once a young man," for Jesus Christ is the God child, the God youth, the God man, the God of all ages. Strive to fulfil with diligence and joy the work of each day, be gay, *very* gay. The life of a true Christian should be a perpetual jubilee, a prelude to the festivals of eternity.

"I want you to do one thing for my sake, and that is for a few minutes each day to read and meditate on one or two verses of the xiv., xv., xvi., and xvii. chapters of St. John's Gospel. It is our Lord's last sermon to man, and every letter is as a precious pearl. Pray every day, in the words of Solomon, for wisdom and understanding. 'Deus patrum nostrorum et Domine misericordiæ, qui omnia fecisti verbo tuo! da mihi sedium tuarum assistricem Sapientiam, quia servus tuus sum ego et filius ancillæ tuæ; homo infirmus et exigui temporis, minor ad intellectum judicii: mitte illam de cœlis sanctis tuis, ut mecum sit et mecum laboret ut sciam quid acceptum sit apud te . . . et faciam. Amen.'

"God accepted Solomon's prayer, and why not ours? And in what consists wisdom? You will find out later."

These letters abundantly show the anxious care and thought which Théophane bestowed on his brothers, who were, besides the continual subject of his prayers, and when he became a priest, of his Masses likewise. On one occasion he wrote and told him that he was going to say Mass for him on the 1st of August, the Feast of St. Eusebius, when, from some unknown reason, he changed it to the *second* of the month. Now it happened on that very day that a thunderbolt struck the College of

Montmorillon, and an electric spark fell on Eusebius, who was left for dead, and with great difficulty recovered. So that he always attributed his escape to the intervention of his brother, who at that very moment was offering up for him the Holy Sacrifice.

To his elder brother, Henry, Théophane writes in a different strain; but his letters are full of suggestive thoughts and beautifully expressed. On one occasion he writes,—

"I am not astonished that my loving old brother found my letters poetical, but I think that his own heart supplied it. Talking of poetry, do you not think that men have profaned it more than ever in these latter days? Poetry presupposes a soul lifted above the things of sense; it means the outpouring of a heart full of love of God and his neighbour, and keenly alive to the beauties of nature and of grace. The mysteries of Christianity and of the Blessed Eucharist are eminently fitted for a poet. So is also pure love, devotion, heroism, self-sacrifice, and the rest. But when I see men calling themselves poets abusing their gift by impure allusions and vile sophistries, and vague aspirations after unreal dreams which have no existence but in their morbid imaginations, I confess I have no patience with them. Poetry is not meant to be merely the exaltation and feeding of human passion and sensual indulgence. And yet three parts of the world call this poetry. Oh, let us draw our inspirations from purer sources! The literature of the day seems to me to run for ever either in impure or rationalistic channels. So much so, that I dread lest we should be all submerged in the foul tide! I try and think of the exile going back to his country. *He sees and thinks of nothing else.* We are all exiles here below. Let us hasten on to our home in Heaven.

..... I am very much struck with the young
men I have met here unconnected with the Seminary. They are such contradictory creatures. A
good deal of pride with a good deal of generosity;
a great love of independence with a certain submission; a great deal of impurity with a vestige of
better thoughts learned at their mother's knee;
some courage and audacity, and yet more weakness
and foolish yielding; an ardour for work by fits
and starts, but in general inconceivable idleness;
a desultory way of living and acting without aim
or purpose; in fact, the old strife between the
spirit of evil and the spirit of good. But amongst
these young men there are exceptions. I know
some living in the world, in the very centre of the
greatest riches and luxury, yet humble, pious,
devout, charitable, reverent, seeking out the poor
in their garrets, religious 'as a woman,' as the
saying is. Their manners are simple and natural,
for they are thoroughly in earnest. They are
bright, amiable, and courteous, with faces which
prepossess one at first sight. All their lives are
spent in doing good. I don't mean to say they
don't commit faults sometimes, for human nature is
weak; but their very failings increase their humility
and make them lean more completely on the Divine
mercy. God be praised. Such men are not very
rare, though they do not show themselves much in
the streets. There is another species, whom one sees
all day long lounging at cafés or in ball-rooms, never
by themselves. They are restless, walking in a wild
sort of way, judging and criticizing every body and
every thing. They neither respect nor esteem women.
They want to know every thing, hear every thing,
see every thing. They talk for the sake of talking,
and their least sin is that of doing nothing. .....
Such young men swarm in the streets of Paris, and

their secret lives are more pitiable than their public ones. All young men, more or less, may rank in one or other of these two classes. It does not cost more to side with the right, but then one must have a heart; and reason calmly as to the object of life; in a word, serve and love God.

"Good-bye, my dearest brother. Do write to me soon again. Your letters do me so much good."

But it was to Mélanie that Théophane spoke of all his most intimate thoughts and aspirations. Poor Mélanie, who had never recovered her brother's departure, and at last had become seriously ill. After a time she rallied, and then her brother (whom she called her "other half") wrote to her as follows:—

"MY DEAREST SISTER,—I am glad you have been ill, and I am very thankful you have recovered. To explain my first proposition, which will appear very extraordinary, I feel that you have had the opportunity to suffer something for the love of our Lord. Oh, I am quite sure you felt the advantages of your position! Sufferings are the money with which one buys Heaven; therefore, your fortune is already begun. As for me, I have not a penny. I am as poor as a church mouse. But I hope soon to go to California. Now do you understand my meaning? Anyhow, you know how I love you."

Mélanie had long wished to devote herself to God in a religious life, but her brother's plans had thwarted the accomplishment of her own wishes for a time. She had made the sacrifice generously. Nevertheless, she felt herself strongly urged in the same direction.

"Be comforted, my dearest sister," writes Théophane, "we are made to live together, so let us do so in Heaven. Be patient until God opens the way for you to give yourself entirely to Him. Perfection does not lie in one state of life more than the other, but consists in an entire correspondence with grace in the position in which God has placed us. Above all, do not be discouraged, or give way to sadness and despondency. Your holy and hidden life in the bosom of your family is quite as meritorious in the sight of God, and perhaps safer than a more heroic one."

But although Mélanie was compelled to wait for a few years to attain the great object of her wishes, she found she could realize a portion of them by devoting her virginity to our Lord, even while still living in the world; and on this she writes to consult her brother. He replies,—

"Your letter has filled me with great joy, for I see how anxious you are to advance in the paths of perfection, and how our Lord has filled you with His grace. I bless and praise Him for it every day, and I beseech Him still further to illuminate your understanding, to strengthen you with His all-powerful grace, to guide you on your upward path, to fill you with the spirit of humility and purity, and to pour upon you the sevenfold gifts of His Holy Spirit; the gift of wisdom, to know and understand God; the gift of intelligence, to discern what is His will; the gift of counsel, to inspire you with prudence; the gift of strength, to overcome your natural weakness; the gift of science, to enlighten your ignorance; the gift of piety, to fill you with His love; the gift of fear, to watch over the secret springs of your heart. I have joined my poor prayers with yours and laid them at the feet of our Lady of Victories. Do nothing hastily. You say you wish to obey your director, and you are quite right, for obedience alone is a sure guide. You are very good to wish to consult me, my dear little sister; I, who am so far below you in every thing! But I thank you with all my heart for this fresh proof of your love. Well! what answer am I to give you? You would not like me to say 'No,' and I should like it still less. How can I advise you to remain in a world which I detest as you do, and which I have left myself? I know well that for a long time you have entirely detached yourself from its pleasures and its frivolities; but the last act, the act of entire renunciation, you have not yet signed, and that is all that is left for you to do. What is there, then, to stop you? Consult your courage, consult the voice of grace, consult those with whom you live, and if no obstacle present itself, may your holy desires be fulfilled. May God's will be done; celebrate your nuptials, give Him your heart and your life, clothe yourself with the nuptial robe, place His ring on your finger, take a new name, enter into a new family. I wish you joy, sister *Mary*, virgin spouse of Jesus Christ! May the day come when I shall see my much-loved sister in the choir of virgins, of which Mary Immaculate is the Queen, and when you shall count your brother in the ranks of apostles, and perhaps martyrs—who knows? How joyfully we shall each then sing, '*Regina Apostolorum, Regina Virginum, ora pro nobis.*' . . . .

"You want me to guess the new name you have taken. I have puzzled my brains in vain, and can find only my own. Perhaps, in the eccentricity of your love, you have chosen that one? And now you say you want to be a missionary-nun—a tertiary, I suppose? I have a little bit of a doubt as to the reality of this vocation; it seems to me to taste a little too much of fraternal affection."

But the great day came for Mélanie, and on the 15th July, 1852, her brother wrote again,—

"I received your cake on the Feast of St. John,

you naughty little spoiling sister, and thought it very good, though a little salt, which is the fault of your confections. Well, be the salt of the earth! So many souls get insipid and lukewarm. Ah, you did not expect me to preach morality to you on a cake! . . . It is just like you and your love to remember all the little details of that last day, and how I carried my surplice on my arm. Ah, I am sometimes afraid you care for me too much! Perhaps it is to punish us both that God told me to leave you. I congratulate you with all my heart on the step you have taken, and that you should thus have separated yourself from the world, though still living in it. God has inspired you, and given you a great grace. I know you will receive it with gratitude and humility; but do not forget that your first duty is still to your family and for your family. . . . God bless you, sister *Mary-Théophane.* All joy be with you in the hearts of Jesus and Mary.—Your devoted brother,
"T. V."

The hour drew near when Théophane was to become a priest, and his zeal and fervour were redoubled. The atmosphere around him strengthened all these pious desires, and every thing tended to help him onward in the path of perfection. In one of the corners of the garden at the Paris Foreign Missionary College is a little oratory dedicated to Our Lady, and filled with candles and flowers. Every Saturday evening, and on all the vigils of her feasts, it is lit up, and the students go there to recite Litanies and sing hymns in her honour, after which follow the usual prayers at nine o'clock. But on leaving the chapel, and before retiring to his cell, each of the future missionaries goes to pay a little visit to the Hall of Martyrs, round which are ranged, not only the relics of the confessors, but the instruments of their torture and pictures of their martyrdom. Every one stays a few minutes here to pray in silence, and then kiss the crucifix stained with the blood of Mgr. Borié. Théophane used to spend every spare moment in this room, and when the news came of the martyrdom of M. Schoeffler at Tonquin, he wrote to his sister, "Oh, if I might some day give my life like him for the Faith! I am not afraid of saying so to you, because I know your generosity, and that you would not even wish to rob me of my crown. This Tonquin Mission is now the most enviable, for it almost certain martyrdom. . . . Whatever happens, I know I may reckon on your prayers."

Every day he was getting more detached. Writing to the Bishop of Poictiers, he says,—

"Formerly, my Lord, I rejoiced in the thought of receiving at your hands the last great grace which God has deigned to bestow on me. But Divine Providence has ordered it otherwise, and disposed of my future. In the midst of my regrets I cannot help looking forward with joy. Yes, I own that every day I get more detached from France, even when France means to me Poictiers, and my tastes have become decidedly Chinese. I do not know what secret impulse makes me sympathize so warmly with people of another clime, be they Indians or Chinese. Some of my friends here declare I am growing like them, that I have a Chinese head, and Chinese eyes, and Chinese ways, in fact, that I am getting Chinese altogether. Do not think, however, that I have set my heart upon China. I have no other choice than the will of my superiors; that is, if they think me worthy of any work at all, which I sometimes fear they will not.

I shall always find myself too happy in the place where the Great Master will allow me to work for the welfare of my brethren, and the Glory of His holy name."

Nevertheless, his superiors had no difficulty in recognizing the eminent merits of the young aspirer after the Foreign Missions, in spite of the humility which induced him to throw a veil over all his actions; and so they hastened the time of his consecration (he was only twenty-two), and desired him to prepare himself for the Trinity Ordination. He received the news with a mixture of joy and fear, and writing to his Bishop exclaims,—

"My Lord,—Fruit which grows ripe before the proper time has no flavour; and here am I, a young and green fruit, which yet must be ripe in a month. In spite of this hot May sun, is it not too soon? .. I never dreamt of being called to the priesthood before Christmas, but God has disposed things otherwise... '*Introibo ad altare Dei, ad Deum qui lætificat juventutem meam.*' Very soon, perhaps, another message will be brought to me, at the very thoughts of which my heart sings for joy. 'Pack up your things, and start.' Yet when I look at myself, when I see the childish hands which are so soon to receive the holy oils; the feet fresh from the playgrounds which are to carry so far the gospel of truth and peace; my whole being, in fact, which is only just beginning to understand what life is, and yet is so soon to teach men how to live, I can scarcely help laughing and yet crying. So mingled are my feelings and thoughts at this moment, I can only hope in God, and beseech Him to give me strength, meekness, humility, prudence, knowledge, and charity. I trust in your lordship's kindness that you will give me a place in your prayers, which will obtain for me the graces of which I stand so much in need."

A severe illness prostrated him for a time, although his courage and cheerfulness never deserted him ; and in spite of his sufferings, which were very great, his gaiety and patience astonished his companions, who vied with one another as to who should wait upon him and do little things for him. He wrote gaily after his recovery, " I have got a new body altogether, which, as I am going into a new country, will be very useful, and I hope we shall agree perfectly. It is only a pity I can't get a new spirit and a new heart, and then I should be altogether a new man. Pray that I may be thus transformed on the day of my ordination." He recovered sufficiently to be ordained on the 5th June, and said his first Mass the next day, being Trinity Sunday. He writes home on this occasion to his father, " My dearest Father,—Send me your blessing. I said my first Mass to-day. Oh, what a glorious day for me ! True, I cannot yet meditate very well—my head is still weak, and I can scarcely realize the awful mysteries of which I have become, as it were, a participator. But I feel a great peace, and am very happy. You will share in my joy, which is a family one. Would that you could have been with me on this day! But God ordered it otherwise. May we be strengthened in faith and hope; at least we shall be united in prayer."

The new missionary was at length a priest. His departure could not be long delayed, and the announcement was made to him three days only after his ordination. He gave notice to his belongings that his destination was not yet fixed, nor the actual day of farewell, but that they must be prepared for a speedy summons. He told them that he had been promised a month's notice, and added, "Dearest Friends,—Courage and faith! God watches over us, and the Blessed Virgin is our protector."

The mission of his two friends, M. Dallet and M. Theurel, was already fixed; the latter was bound for Tonquin, the former for India. M. Dallet embarked in the middle of the month of August, and this was the first break in the chain which united these faithful friends.

But the summons for our fervent missionary was not long delayed, and a letter dated the 13th of September announced his speedy departure to his family.

"MY DEAREST FATHER, MÉLANIE, HENRY, AND EUSEBIUS,—Once more let us say together, God's holy name be praised! About a month ago five of my fellow-students received a notice to hold themselves in readiness for departure. I was left behind until my health was more re-established. I could not help grieving very much, but let that pass, for time presses. One of the five, who had been compelled to return home for family affairs, did not come back on the day fixed. I have been, consequently, appointed to replace him. I am, therefore, going to leave you at once, dearest people, and to wish you good-bye until our reunion in Heaven. I shall not remain even this week in Paris; Friday will probably be my last day on the soil of France, as we are to embark at Antwerp."

The 19th of September was to be the day of departure, and in the morning the fervent missionary sent a farewell line to each member of his family.

"MY DEAREST AND MUCH-LOVED FATHER,—To-day I leave France. To-day I must send you my last farewell; we start at seven o'clock. On Monday we are to embark from Antwerp; Tuesday morning we set sail. Dearest father, good-bye. My departure I know will be a sorrow to you; to me also the separation is very hard to bear. But courage! Life on earth passes so quickly, and death will reunite us so soon; for death to a Christian is life, a life of eternal happiness in the bosom of our God, in company with His angels and His saints. *Au revoir*, then, dearest father; the way is short, and the end is blessed. Good-bye, I embrace you with all my heart."

"MY MUCH-LOVED SISTER, MY OWN LITTLE MÉLANIE,—Good-bye. I feel very much not being able to write you a good long letter. It is positive suffering to me, for we have so many, many things to say to each other, but I have scarcely a moment. I shall never forget you or our happy childhood together, or our family gatherings and home joys, but by and by we shall all be reunited. I go with a heavy heart and eyes full of tears, but we must pray together, the one for the other, and bear the pain of parting bravely. God bless you. My paper must convey my last kiss to my darling sister."

"Good-bye, my dear, good Henry. Your last letter gave me so much pleasure. Oh no, my heart is not made of stone; on the contrary, just now it melts like wax. But we shall meet again. I am going to talk of our Father who is in Heaven, and make Him known to our brothers who as yet know Him not, and perhaps I shall be first at the tryst. Pray for me. Prayer alone can soften bitterness and soothe sorrow. And I, do you think I can ever forget you? Good-bye. Let us have courage in this life and fight our battles bravely. I love you with all my heart."

"Good-bye, my poor little Eusebius. We are about to be separated, but we shall be more and more closely united in thought and prayer. We must all walk straight heavenwards, no matter how rough the way. Happy those who get there first! My colleagues and I start under the best auspices, for only yesterday we heard of a fresh martyrdom in Tonquin, and it is for that mission we are bound. Good-bye! I kiss you on both cheeks. Once more, good-bye!"

Then came the usual service for their departure, which, though it has been often described, we venture to repeat here. They were brought into the chapel after evening prayers, and knelt on the steps of the altar. Behind them knelt the Directors of the College, and the other students, as well as their friends and relations who came to see them for the last time, although Théophane's were not of the number. After the prayers were over, a short meditation was given, and then the assistants sat down, and the five missionaries alone remained standing on the altar-step, while one of the Directors, who had himself lately returned from the Foreign Missions, made them a short but touching address. Then the five young Apostles went up to the altar, and when close to the tabernacle turned round to their brethren, who, leaving their places, went one by one, and kissed the feet of those who were so soon to be our Lord's heralds, whilst the choir intoned the anthem, "*Quam speciosi pedes evangelizantium pacem, evangelizantium bona!*"

A little episode followed, which was well described by an eminent Catholic writer.

"In the midst of the crowd of visitors an old man came forward, walking with some difficulty, and assisted by one of the Directors of the College. An inexpressible emotion was felt throughout the chapel, and the voices of the choir faltered as they watched him slowly advancing up the aisle towards the altar. He kissed the feet of the four first missionaries, but when he came to the fifth, the young man, as if instinctively, bent forward and tried to prevent him. But the poor old man knelt, or rather prostrated himself before him, and not only pressed his lips to his feet, but his face and his forehead, so that his soft white hair covered them as with a veil; and then a sigh burst from his heart, which was more like a sob, a sigh which was heard all over the building, and at which every body was moved to tears; while the poor son himself (for it was his father) became whiter than a sheet. Yet this was the second son which this new Abraham had sacrificed to God, and it was the last! . . . . They assisted the old man to rise, and he with difficulty returned to his place amidst the sympathy of the whole audience, while the choir, who in the excitement had paused for a moment, intoned the "*Laudate pueri Dominum.*"

After this touching ceremony, the missionaries themselves gave the kiss of peace to their brethren and friends, and then followed the "*Hymn of departure,*" by M. Dallet, which we give in the Appendix.

CHAPTER V.

OUR travellers left Paris and the Seminary with full hearts. To Théophane, especially, the parting was very bitter, for he had become attached to the

College, and to every thing in it, in a way which
only clinging, loving natures like his can understand. They contrived to get together in the railway carriage, so that they might mutually console
one another; and after a time they became calm,
and even joyous, so that Théophane wrote "that
they seemed more like people going to a fête."
Arrived at Antwerp they lost no time in going on
board their ship, the "Phylotaxe" (lover of order),
an American clipper of 600 tons, and a good and
fast sailer. A day or two elapsed before the ship
was ready for sea, which they spent in seeing this
quaint old Belgian town, and admiring both the
simplicity and devotion of its inhabitants. The
embarkation took place on the 23rd September.
Théophane wrote home,—

"We bid farewell to Antwerp with a salute of
nine guns, which was answered from the citadel.
I am rather inclined to dreaming, and were it not
for the help of God my heart would fail me altogether. You were more than half of my life, and
I feel the separation most terribly; and especially
from the fact that it may be so long before I shall
have any letter or tidings of you all. But at any
rate you are *anchored* in my remembrance (you see I
am already getting nautical in my expressions), and
I feel as if your presence would be ever with me,
to cheer and strengthen me. We have already
passed two nights on board; how beautiful the
nights are at sea! The moon throws such a soft
light on the waves while we walk up and down the
deck, singing some national air, and smoking our
cigars. For now we are *ordered* to smoke; and a
kind old gentleman at Antwerp gave me a thousand cigars for the passage, of a mild kind, which
I can manage better than the stronger ones. I
sleep like a little bird in its nest, and as yet I have

not been sick. The vessel is most comfortable; the wind favourable; the crew a picked one; the discipline admirable, and the captain beloved like a father. In spite of the dispensation, we abstained on the Friday, as it is the universal Belgium custom. The captain never omits grace before and after meals, and the officers do the same. I am struck with the hardness of the lives of these sailors, but I see it has a certain charm. I like hearing their monotonous singing during their work, and watching them climbing the ropes; but the wonderful expanse of water all round one, and the thoughts which it suggests, occupy me almost exclusively. I wished good-bye to every village and steeple as we sailed by. Now we see nothing but sky and sea. Good-bye, then, for many months." He was enabled, however, to send a few pencil lines the next day, as follows:—

"*Sunday, September* 26, *by a Fishing-Smack, seven leagues from Calais.*

"DEAR FRIENDS,—One more word to say that I am well, though rather sea-sick. We are all bright and cheery on board. Pray for us. Dearest Father, Mélanie, Henry, Eusebius, once more good-bye! A last farewell to France, and to you all."

According to all human probability these were, indeed, the last words he was to send them from Europe; but a further consolation was granted to his family through a violent gale, which obliged their ship to take refuge in Plymouth harbour, where they remained three days. Théophane gave his brother an amusing account of the storm and its consequences; and adds, "This evening I have been watching a beautiful sunset on the English coast, whilst the moon was rising on the

French side of the Channel. I could not help reflecting upon England, that country where the Sun of Truth has so long been darkened; and praying for her with all my heart. England could do so much for the good cause, if she would only make it her own! If she only saw the truth! She reigns over the seas; but she only sows error wherever her flag floats. Let us pray that this state of things may not continue. It is, I fancy, a rare sight for English people to see a priest in his cassock; for when we went into the town, men, women, and children looked at us in amazement. Some of the little ones were fairly frightened, and ran away, and one of the men was curious enough to come and touch one of our cassocks and examine the buttons. Then they burst out laughing, and that so naively, that we laughed too. It seems to me that they are very like the Chinese in character—curious to the verge of incivility, and with little sense in their mockery."

To his sister he wrote,—

"PLYMOUTH.

"DEAREST SISTER,—Peace and love and joy in our Lord Jesus Christ. Providence has willed that we should be detained here, to repair the damage done to our ship in the gale—at least, that is the reason the world gives; *I* believe it is to enable me once more to say good-bye at my ease to my friends. What do you think, dear little sister? Do you recollect how in old times, when the last days of the holidays came, you and I used to take the longest road to the station, so as to prolong the time as much as possible and talk a little more? We never could agree as to which was to have the last word; we always had so much to say to each other. And now I am leaving

you indeed, and probably for ever! Ought we
not, then, to have a good long talk? Ah, now
comes the sorrow! I must have all the say to
myself. There is no dear little Mélanie to answer
me; no gentle eyes to look at me; no soft hand to
hold in mine, and to keep it back, and try to make
me stay a few minutes longer! And our good
father and brother, where are they? Ah, you are
all together; and I? I am alone! Alone with God—
alone for evermore! But I know how you have
followed me in thought; and I like to think of
this letter's arrival at our home, and the welcome
it will get! Am I not a real baby? But O my
God, it is not wrong, is it? to love one's home, and
one's father, and one's brothers, and one's sister?
—to suffer terribly at being parted from them?—
to feel one's loneliness?—to try and console one
another?—to mingle our prayers and our tears,
and also our hopes? For we have left all for
Thee. We wish to work but for Thee; and we
trust to be reunited one day in Thee for ever and
for ever! You see, my darling sister, as usual, I
cannot help opening my whole heart to you, who
understand me so well. But let us look the thing
bravely in the face. *All is over*, is it not so? An
enormous distance is about to separate us. Never
again shall we meet on this earth! But after all,
why is it we feel it so dreadfully? A little sooner
or a little later, we shall be together again in
Heaven. How short will our separation appear to
us in eternity! Our mother, our friends, the
SAINTS, are all gone home before us. *Au revoir!* they said. So it is our business to follow
them, and to go to them. People who are taking
a journey often go different roads—one one way,
the other another: the only question is, which
shall arrive first at the place of destination.

Well, I am going by this road; you by that.
Let the one who reaches home first encourage the
other.

"Mélanie, my sister, I leave you a precious
charge—that of our dear old father! You must
help him to pass from this world to a better. You
must be his angel of consolation, and soothe his
last days on earth. Watch over our brothers, too;
try and make yourself one with them as you have
been with me; and link yourself with them in the
bonds of the tenderest affection. Three are stronger
than one; help one another onwards and upwards
in the rugged path of life. Above all, let nothing
separate your interests or your affections. True
love cannot be snapped asunder; it spreads and
widens, but never diminishes. Love never dies;
for it is stronger than death. God Himself has
said so. The strength and increase of love is in
prayer. We are little and weak and miserable,
but He who sustains us is strong and mighty. His
arms are ever stretched out towards us; let us lift
up ours to meet Him.

"Life has many bitter, sad, and weary hours;
often it can scarcely be called existence. The
little rivulets, as well as the great rivers, all empty
themselves into one source—the sea. God is an
ocean of love and mercy; in Him alone is the
fulness of joy. Patience and courage, then! A
little while, and we shall be with Him. He has
promised it, and He never belies His word. When
the little river is dried up, the heavens give rain,
and the river gaily continues its course. When
our life is arid, and we are ill at ease, let us ask
for the dew and the refreshing rain and the food
from God. Our Father who is in Heaven knows
our wants, and feels for our weariness; and He
sends His ministers to supply our need. 'Ask, and

ye shall have.' Well, then, it is an understood thing, that each one of us is to help and strengthen the other, and to make a start upwards. Short is the way, and short is the time. Courage, dearest sister! my thoughts press and tumble one upon the other; but you understand even a half word; and you will make the others enter into my feelings. I can only speak freely to you; but if I write confusedly you will unravel it.

"Dear Mélanie, when you hear the priest at mass intone the '*Sursum corda,*' think that it is I who am speaking to you, I who invite you in our dear Lord's name to lift up your heart. Yes, mount upwards! upwards! Mount always, like a bird of passage; and then all this sorrow will assume its just proportions, and Heaven will be attained. Even on this sad earth, with hearts on high, and spade in hand, we must labour on, each at his task. Be patient, gentle, loving; and pray for me, that I, working in my little furrow, may be the same. Pray for those among whom I am going to work; for these poor heathen brothers and sisters of ours, for whom I would so gladly give my life. Make your prayers thoroughly Catholic in that sense, for that is the real meaning of the communion of saints.

"From time to time I hope you will write me long letters to cheer me in my solitude; and that you will beg our dear old friends to do the same. Think what a joyful surprise a letter will be to me out there! I shall send my scribblings in a Chinese guise to make you laugh; for we must try and be gay and bright in our correspondence, and not dwell always on the sadder side of life. And now, my darling sister, I must come to a stop. There is a limit to every thing, even to these closely-written pages! My heart rests on your heart, and my hand in yours. À Dieu. You understand? God bless you, my dearest sister!"

From Plymouth Théophane wrote also a few lines to his little brother:—
"Bless our Lord, and the rain, and the winds and the tempests which have blown me into this town of Plymouth, so that I might write one word more to my dear little Eusebius! Our good-bye has been said, and our lives will henceforth run in different channels; unless you come to have a Chinese taste like me! I turn my back upon you, but not my heart, you will understand! Our thoughts will ever be united, in our prayers as in our work. You are going back to college. Work! work! work! Time is more precious than you can have an idea of. Learn all you possibly can, but especially languages; for people fraternize a great deal more than they used to do, and this fusion should tend to the triumph of truth. Try and co-operate in this great work. I leave you to the care of your good angel. May he guard and protect your youth and your whole life! Dear brother, we shall see one another in Heaven. I give you for advice the same words as Mélanie, '*Sursum corda.*' May God give you the fulness of His grace, patience, peace, and joy, in life and death! Amen."

These letters were dated the 7th of October. Two days after, the voyagers left the port of Plymouth, and no news were received of them till the month of April following, when a letter arrived from Singapore, dated February. He wrote a long and detailed account of the passage, with which we will not weary our readers, as all long voyages resemble one another. But we will give a few of the personal details which bear upon his character and feelings:—

"We are entering the harbour, so I will prepare my home letters, and am glad to do so on New Year's Day. This morning my first thought after God was for you all. On the 10th October, being Sunday evening, we left Plymouth. Another Belgian vessel, the 'Atalanta,' left the port at the same time, with 160 passengers who were going to the gold-fields. What a poor object! You may believe that not for all the gold in Australia or California would I have left you all! Our vessel is a very fast sailer, and our captain a model of all virtues, religious from conviction, speaking little, but always to the point; he has his ship in perfect order, but is immensely beloved by his men; and his courtesy and kindness towards us could not be exceeded. The days are long and monotonous on board ship; a few strange birds, one or two swallows, flying-fish, and porpoises, with a shark here and there, those are the only events in a long voyage. The sea, I confess, wearies me to death. It is certainly a fine sight to see great waves rolling one over another, or to contemplate the immense extent of water on every side, but I should prefer seeing it from *terra firma*. We had the unspeakable consolation of daily mass for the first month and a half; but afterwards our altar-breads got spoiled. Oh, how I have longed for the possibility of paying a visit to the Blessed Sacrament, or once more of assisting at some Catholic ceremony! When the body is deprived of food, it languishes and dies; and it is the same with the soul, without the bread which sustains its life. . . . Often and often I found myself dreaming on the deck, leaning against the bulwarks, and looking back on my past life—on my happy childhood, on my darling mother, on my father's sacrifices for my education, on our joyous home gatherings, on my life at school and at college..... And now here I am, in the hands of Providence, full of thankfulness for past mercies and blessings, full of hope for the future. My dear father, in your last letter, consenting to my departure, you encouraged me by saying, 'The hand of God is every where.' This shall henceforth be my motto. The hand of God is every where; therefore it will be every where with me. Holy confidence, then, trust and hope for you and for me, and for us all..... On our arrival at Singapore we heard of the proclamation of the empire without much astonishment. God grant peace to our dear France! In this country it seems to me that gold is the supreme god. New mines are daily discovered; but I never heard that they found in them peace or happiness. No; it is charity alone which is pure gold, gold tried in the furnace; the rest is but false money."

Our missionaries were still at Singapore when several young Cochin-Chinese students arrived who had been sent by Mgr. Gaultier to the College of Penang. The sight of them made Théophane's heart beat quicker than ever, and he wrote to Father Dallet,—

"Every evening these young men pray together in their own language, and we put our ears to the cracks of the door to hear them. And then their singing is so sweet! Such plaintive, touching tones! And shall I tell you all? They are real heroes that we have next to us. Men on whose heads a price has been put for leaving their country. They are the sons, the brothers of martyrs, and they come from Annam, the land of martyrdoms."

After spending three weeks at Singapore, M. Vénard and two of his companions started for Hong Kong. The rest remained a few days longer, till a favourable opportunity presented itself for going to their respective destinations. Before leaving Singapore, Théophane wrote a few lines to the great friend and companion of his boyhood, a young lady living near his old home :—

"I like to think that you remember our old walks on the hill side, and the pleasant readings we used to have together. I assure you I have a faithful memory, and I never can think of those happy days without emotion. All my friends have a place in my heart, and the thought of them often brings tears to my eyes; not that I regret what I have done, for it seems to me that I simply followed the inspiration of God's grace, but because this separation from those so dear to me cannot take place without a terrible wrench; and when the wound is reopened it bleeds.

"You tell me you are full of troubles and trials. I can well believe it; and I ask of God to give you strength and grace to bear them. You know how deeply interested I am in every thing that concerns you. Ah, one cannot but own that life on this earth is a poor thing at best, and that there is scarcely a day without a cloud! Sorrow and suffering are found every where; they are the daily bread of each one of us. The thing is to know how to use them. Happy those who know how to turn them to advantage! Such souls will be amply recompensed hereafter. I always look upon these miseries as a kind of money with which to buy Heaven; but then this money must bear the image of Jesus Christ, just as our ordinary coinage bears the superscription of the king or queen of the country where it is struck. Courage, then, courage! One King loves you and calls you to Himself by His own way, the royal road of the Cross. Try to love it for His sake, and to follow

Him gladly, when and where He calls you. When we shall meet each other again in the place where we all hope to be reunited, you will be rich in glory, for you have been rich in sorrows and in merits!"

From Singapore our missionary proceeded to Hong Kong, where he arrived after a long and tedious passage on board an English sailing-ship. The joy which he felt on landing made him exclaim, "I feel all the more keenly how great a rest it will be to quit this stormy sea of the world, and repose in our good God!" He was a little disappointed at not finding at Hong Kong the letters which were to fix his future destination; but he consoled himself with the thought, which his humility was ever ready to suggest, that he was not yet fit for the heavy charge of the Apostolate. A still keener disappointment arose from finding no home letters—not even one from his sister! He felt this hard, and his loneliness pressed upon him heavily for the first few weeks. When tidings from his family at last arrived, he broke forth into a song of joy to his father, as follows:—

"Oh, your letters did me so much good! I love them as one loves the dew after great heats; as the traveller in the desert rejoices at the green oasis where his camels and himself can rest and find shade and water. For we poor missionaries live, as it were, in a desert, and that always. When we get news of our loved ones at home, of our country, of our friends, how happy it makes us! I feel a thousand times stronger when I have read and re-read your dear letters, for your sympathy fortifies and encourages me. I no longer feel alone in my sacrifice: others share in it and live, as it were, with me in thought and heart. God be praised for the home love in which I have been cradled, and for the dear friends He has given me! I am as a branch of a tree, and no longer dried up by being separated from the parent stem, for the same loving sap runs through us all. After all, God is very good to our human hearts, which He has formed, and of which He knows the yearnings and the weaknesses; and then He is the same in China as in France, and what do we want beside Him on earth or in Heaven!"

M. Vénard stayed fifteen months at Hong Kong, during which time he devoted himself to learning the Chinese language, in itself a most arduous and wearisome task; for the different dialects are innumerable, and although he put all his heart into it, yet his health, which was affected by the great heat, often prevented his studying. When that was the case he used to take long walks by the sea-shore or in the mountains, trying to become acquainted with the people and their habits; and although their hypocrisy and egotism often disgusted him, still the modesty of the women, and their careful decency in dress and manner, often contrasted favourably with the customs of his own countrywomen. The thing which drove him to despair was the bad example given to the natives by Europeans calling themselves Christians, who, as he expressed it, "wherever they went, spoilt God's work." But his special indignation was roused by the conduct of the English regarding the opium trade. He writes to his sister,—

"This opium is a substance extracted from the poppy, and which is smoked like tobacco. The result is a positive destruction of all the faculties of mind and body, ending in complete stupefaction. The Chinese have a passion for this pernicious drug, and the English an equal anxiety to supply them with it; they bring it from Hindostan. In spite of treaties and protestations, the sums acquired in this contraband traffic are enormous, and the trade is a thorough disgrace to the English nation. If the devil had tried to have invented something which should ruin men, body and soul, he could not have hit upon any thing more effectual. I wish we could have an association of prayers, to try and put down this infamous traffic."

Writing to M. Dallet, on the Chinese insurrection, he says, " Nothing can be more terrible at this moment than the state of China. But the melancholy thing is that European agents are at the bottom of it, and vainly imagine, by coquetting with the rebels, to promote a Protestant movement among the people. Never was there such a delusion! Not that I wonder at this offspring of Protestantism, for as it is the father of Freemasonry and secret societies, and revolution throughout Europe, under the guise of liberty, so here it engenders a like spirit. We can say to them as our Saviour did of the Jews, ' *Vos ex patre diabolo estis, et desideria patris vestri vultis facere.*' The worst of it is that it all adds to the hatred of the Chinese towards strangers; so that when the Emperor succeeds in defeating the rebels, which is inevitable, his vengeance will fall on the Europeans, and especially on the missionaries. . . . . You ask me, ' What are the rebels about?' Nobody knows. The French and English papers write long articles, and give their readers astounding intelligence of battles fought and won, and develope grand theories as to the future of the Chinese Empire; but they are all the dreams of editors. Every one laughs at them here, for there is not a word of truth in their statements; and as to the marvellous changes which this rebellion is to bring about, I think they will find that the mountain has brought forth a mouse!

They talk, too, of the energetic representations made by the French and English ministers in favour of Christianity; all this is pure invention. The spirit of Constantine and of St. Louis is far from being that of modern Governments, which have all become more or less atheistical under the influence of Protestant, rationalistic, and infidel doctrines; expediency is their watchword. As for us, in God alone is our hope and succour. Let us pray, then, more and more fervently for the conversion of the infidels."

The numbers of letters which we find written by Théophane to his old friend, M. Dallet, prove that their affection had not been cooled by distance or separation. We give an extract from one written on the 26th of September, 1853:—

"You ask me, dear old friend, if you live as much as ever in my remembrance? Oh yes, quite as much! I love you with a special and devoted attachment, and you must not be scandalized at it. It is surely allowable to have a warm, particular friendship, especially when so far away from its object, and the community will not be the sufferers. I have a full belief and confidence that God does not disapprove of it; for it is in Him and for Him that our hearts have been united. It is not the evil which is in us which unites us in this tender bond of love, but our higher and better aspirations. Let us, then, be for ever *one*, my dearest brother, for ever united in the same work, devoted to the same cause, humble disciples of the same Master. For all the world put together, don't let us look back! I assure you the more intercourse I have with mankind in general, the more they disgust me; and the longer I live, the more bitter and disappointing I find this world. . . . . *Nolite diligere mundum neque ea quæ in mundo sunt*, and who taught me that but you? So let us go on bravely,

with one heart and one mind. Our feet toil painfully here on earth, but our thoughts soar above.
.... *Et mundus transit et concupiscentia ejus; qui autem fecit voluntatem Dei, manet in æternum.* My Bishop wrote to me, just before I left Paris, 'I pray for you to our dear Lord, that your devotion may daily become more perfect, that your holocaust be complete, and that having embarked in so great a work, you may persevere in it after the manner of the saints. *Do not be an Apostle by halves,* my dear child. Having before you the highest models, imitate them in their abnegation, their contempt of life, their practice of the interior life. Thus will you be raised to their level, and multiply the conquests of Jesus Christ.' Now I have these words always before me, and they give me courage and strength; and I have copied them for you that you may use them too. .... I have been laughing at the idea of your beard, of which you fancy I shall be envious; but I assure you my moustache is quite enough for me. .... Dearest friend, I am afraid you are a good deal tried in your present mission. If I were only by your side to grasp your hand, and share all your troubles, as of yore! I know you so well that I feel the more for your peculiar trials. But it is always the same; the gold must pass through the furnace. God will prove and try you, and having fed you with milk, is now weaning you for stronger and greater things. Don't let us be '*Apostles by halves!*' It's a great thing to be a missionary! Our duties are without limit, and imply perfection, if possible. But let us try and realize what it is God requires of us, and when the moment of action comes, let us not be found wanting. All the miseries you picture to me I feel and see vividly, and my heart bleeds for you. But I want you to feel as I do, that all this

which is so painful and displeasing to our poor
human nature works for our good. I feel that my
own soul is strengthened by suffering, and that
from one's very wounds arise greater vigour, firmness, and courage. You tell me of all these sad
things, but you add, 'Happy are those who can
keep themselves apart, and live in the still silence
of their own hearts with God.' Oh, yes, that is
what we must aim after in the midst of all the
trials and vexations which surround us! May God
pour into your wounds the wine and oil which alone
can heal them, and make you taste the sweetness
as well as the bitterness of His cross! '*Bene-
dictus Deus et Pater Domini nostri Jesu Christi, qui
consolatur nos in omni tribulatione nostra!*' . . . .
Some people say, 'Separation, distance; these are
the touchstones of human love and friendship.'
Well, I put my hand on my heart, and I feel it
beats stronger for you than ever; that I love you
almost more than when we were together. You
see our parting was such a real sorrow! Such a
deep wound! But it is the same with every thing.
We love God at heart; we strive and wish to do
so; we love the thoughts of Heaven, and its rest,
and its joys; but it is all a suffering love, for it is
a love in spite of separation. In Paradise there
will be nothing of this pain; but we shall enjoy
the plenitude of the love of God, and of each
other, without tears or partings. Would that that
day were come for us both! Courage, then! The
strife is short after all, and then will be Peace!
Peace! Peace! Do you recollect our discussion
on that word, and of the etymology of Jerusalem,
which we used to end with our favourite hymn,
'*Cœlestis urbs Hierusalem, beata pacis visio*'? . . . .
Well, I must stop. My heart could go on for ever
to you, but my head and hand are tired. I repeat

constantly my favourite little ejaculation for us both. '*Jesu, mitis et humilis corde, miserere nobis!*' In fact, I say them so constantly to myself that they have become a habit. I hear you exclaim, 'Ah, he is going to preach again!' No, for once you are wrong. I am not going to give you any more bad advice, but try and become more humble and amiable myself. God bless you, dearest friend and brother."

Théophane had many warm college friends besides Father Dallet; and among these we must mention the Abbé Theurel, who is now Bishop of Acanthus. These links were never broken till the end, for Théophane looked upon them, as he wrote, "as given by God; and that each soul might be helped upwards by mutual love in the heavenly race." After some weeks spent together at Hong Kong, M. Theurel left for Tonquin, leaving Théophane to follow him later. This separation with the last of his fellow-travellers was very trying to our fervent missionary, who consoled himself by writing certain stanzas in his honour. He had always a great taste and talent for poetry, and used often to say that he had to guard himself, like Father Faber, lest it should absorb him too much. Other friends from the Foreign Missionary College soon joined him, among whom was M. Chapdelaine, who was a good deal older than Théophane, being about forty. He describes him as "a Norman, with an iron constitution, frank, gay, and loyal in character, a capital companion, and especially a holy and courageous missionary." Writing to M. Dallet, he adds, "Father Chapdelaine (who sends you his best love, by-the-bye) is only waiting till his little lodging is prepared to start. He is the healthiest, the most active, and the jolliest of us all; and Father Bariod might well say on his birthday that he had 'the rosiness of perpetual youth.'" After a few years of arduous toil in the mission of Kouang-Si, this joyous, ardent spirit received in 1856 the crown of martyrdom! But we are anticipating. Near the town of Hong Kong a College had been established for the Canton Mission, under the patronage of St. Francis Xavier. M. Guillemin was the head of this College, and he asked M. Vénard to come and teach philosophy to those students who had made their first studies at Penang, which is another Missionary College. Théophane gladly accepted, delighted to have found some definite work during this time of weary waiting, and especially to be under the direction of a man whom every one looked upon as a saint. A few years later this very M. Guillemin came to Europe, was consecrated Bishop at Rome, and then paid a visit to France, bringing with him a young Chinese who had been Théophane's pupil. Eusebius Vénard was then in the Theological Seminary, and described Mgr. Guillemin's visit to Poictiers as follows:—

"It was on the 30th of January, 1857, that Mgr. Guillemin came to the Seminary to talk to us about his mission. The first day I could not get any private conversation with him, but I made acquaintance with Benedict, his Chinese companion, and began talking to him about Théophane. The moment I mentioned his name his whole face lit up with joy, and one saw that it awoke in him the fondest recollections; in fact, from that moment we became like brothers. The next day I was presented to his Grace: he looked at me attentively, and seeing in me a likeness to my brother, exclaimed, 'Oh, my dear Abbé! my good Abbé!' and was much moved. Then he began to talk of Théophane, of his zeal and devotion, of his bright, gay, frank manner, of his distinguished talents, of the way he was beloved, and of his ingenious charity and kindness towards every one. He added, 'When I was made Superior of the Canton Mission, all the students, with Théophane at their head, came to congratulate me, and to recite some verses which he had composed in my honour. He had even made a mitre and crozier of bamboo, with a playful allusion to their being a prophecy of that which they most wished, and to which dignity, unhappily for my poor self, I have now arrived. But this cheerful, bright spirit of his was of immense use to me in directing the College. The students adored him, and he kept up an admirable spirit amongst them, which enabled them to make light of every hardship and difficulty. He went with me one day on an expedition up a high mountain, from whence we could see what he called his 'Promised Land.' Never did I see him so joyous. Ah, your brother is indeed a perfect missionary, and I have done nothing but regret his departure for Tonquin, for I loved him very much, and he belonged to me first of all!' He then gave me a quantity of little details of his daily life, too long to write, but all showing his deep affection for my brother, and his thorough appreciation of his merits."

Théophane's affectionate veneration for his Superiors, and his reverence for Episcopal authority, were strengthened by his own sincere humility, of which the following extract from a letter of his, written from Tonquin to the Bishop of Poictiers, is a proof:—

"I have received the letter which your Grace has deigned to write to me, and which gave me indescribable pleasure, although it filled me with confusion, as therein you call me your *friend*; that I should be your child I understand, but as for the title of friend, I do not dare accept it, I am too young, too little experienced in life, and too unworthy."

It was in the month of February, 1854, that Father Vénard received his orders for the Western district of Tonquin. He wrote at once to express his joy to M. Barran, Superior of the Foreign Missionary College at Paris.

"VERY REV. FATHER SUPERIOR.—Tonquinese for Chinese, I shall not lose much by the exchange! I should have liked any mission which was awarded me; but that of Tonquin, under the care of that great and holy Bishop, Mgr. Retord, so full of holy associations and blessed recollections, oh, this is indeed the post I should most ardently have coveted! I love it as being the heritage which the great Father has awarded to me. I love it because it is the grandest mission of the whole, 'the Diamond of Asia,' as a poet has called it. When I was at Paris, and so unhappy at being left behind, when my brothers had all been sent to their respective destinations, M. Albrand, to console me, said, 'Do not be cast down, this is not a case of *tarde venientibus ossa!*' I like to think of this, and I beg of you to express all my gratitude to that dear, good Father for all his kindness towards me."

Théophane wrote also to his family. "Well, my dear people, I am going to Tonquin. There the venerable Charles Cornay died a martyr. I do not say that the same fate is reserved for me; but if you will only pray ardently, perhaps God may grant me a like grace. . . . I am not going to

China, which I have seen as Moses saw the promised land; but I must guide my boat to another shore, a shore on which MM. Schoeffler and Bonnard (one on the 1st of May, 1851, the other on the 1st of May, 1852) obtained the martyr's palm. It is in the Annamite country, which includes Tonquin and Cochin-China, where the spirit of persecution is most active. A price is put upon the head of each missionary, and when one is found, they put him to death without hesitation. But God knows His own, and only to those whom He chooses is the grace of martyrdom given. The one is taken and the other left, and there as every where His Holy Will is done. In spite of the violence and the universality of the persecution, it is there that the missions are the most flourishing. "*Sanguis martyrum semen Christianorum.*" We run the risk likewise of being cut off by pirates in the passage from Hong Kong to Tonquin; but that must be as God permits. . . . This mission, to which I am appointed, is indeed a grand one! Grand in its organization; grand in the number and fervour of its converts, who amount to upwards of 150,000 souls; grander still in its hopes; grand in its native clergy, who number 80 priests, and 1200 catechists; grand in its religious communities, for there are upwards of 600 sisters; grand in its seminaries, where there are more than 300 students; grand in its chief pastor, of whom the highest praise that can be given is, that since his episcopate, he has added 40,000 sheep to his fold. Is not that a noble escort with which to mount to Heaven? a beautiful crown for all eternity? I cannot tell you with what impatience I am looking forward to being under so holy a bishop, to be initiated by him into the apostolic ministry, to be trained in his school, and to march, as a simple soldier, under the orders of so great a general. There are already six missionaries under him from the Foreign Missionary College. May I make a worthy seventh! And then think of the martyrs,—those real glories of Tonquin, those immortal flowers gathered by our Lord's own hand in the garden of His predilection. These martyrs are the patrons and protectors of the mission; their blood shed in the great cause is always pleading for us before God, and the remembrance of their triumph gives fresh courage to those who are still in the strife. Only think what an honour and what a happiness it would be for your poor Théophane, if God deigned, ·... you understand. '*Te Deum laudamus* .... *Te martyrum candidatus laudat exercitus.*'" He wrote also to his old friend, Father Dallet; and as if martyrdom was the great object of his life, he exclaimed to his friend, "Only a few years ago MM. Galy and Berneux were seized on their arrival at Tonquin; if the same good luck could but befall us! Oh, dear old friend, every time that the thought of martyrdom comes across me, I thrill all over with joy and hope! But then this better part is not given to all. '*Exultent in Domino sancti. Alleluia!*' I dare not aspire to so brilliant a crown, '*Domine, non sum dignus;*' but I cannot help feeling a longing and sighing for such a grace. '*Domine qui dixisti: majorem charitatem nemo habet ut animam suam ponat quis pro amicis suis.*' You do not forget our mutual prayer, it has for me an inexpressible charm: '*Sancta Maria, Regina Martyrum, ora pro nobis!*' Pray, pray for your poor little friend, who never forgets you, no, not for a single day!"

To his brother Henry he wrote, "Ah! how well I understand what you meant when you said,

"Eusebius is arrived fresh and well, so that here we are ALMOST a complete family party." And I, poor little I, on the contrary, am going farther and farther away! Ah! I assure you my thoughts travel back to St. Loup very, very often, and the tears come into my eyes when I think of you all and our happy home, and all the joys of one's childhood and youth. Never since my departure have I known family happiness and real love; such things are not to be met with every day! But I expected it. I felt that it was inevitable. All I can hope is, that after the wound will come the healing. Every age, every position has its cares, its pains, and its bitternesses. Nothing but what comes from God is good here below; but we have much to thank Him for, and especially for the grace which makes us His friends. . . . Do not think of me as sad; on the contrary, I am very happy and bright; when one is working and living for God, one's heart is at ease. And you, you say you are all day scribbling on musty papers. Well, office life has its charms for some. For me, had I not chosen a different path, I should have preferred to work in the fresh air. The day's shooting you tell me of brought back such pleasant recollection of the good old times. I could have fancied myself there! At Tonquin I wonder what I shall find? Not much game, I fancy. Well, one finds our good God every where, and He is our happiness and our joy. There is no use in being sad, so that in the midst of discouragement and disgust, and every kind of mental suffering, one must try and take one's heart in both hands, and force it to cry out, 'Welcome joy all the same!' The soul finds itself in such a different state at different times; some days, gay and calm, and at ease; other days, sad and weary, and broken-hearted. This is the case with every one, unless you are a natural phenomenon! I believe it is the struggle between the upper and lower parts of our nature. When our better half triumphs, we are at peace; but when we let ourselves go, and yield to our natural inclinations, then comes a state of disorder, and of anxiety, and of longing after the impossible, and of dissatisfaction with our lot, and with the position in which God has seen fit to place us; and this state of mind must be vigorously resisted, for it obscures our judgment and falsifies our ideas. Now there are certain things which strengthen the ascendency of evil thoughts in us, and these are bad companions, bad books, a forgetfulness of daily duties, and consequent vicious habits. But of all these, bad books are the worst. They are the plague of the present day. A book is bad not only when it contains impure and immoral thoughts, but when it gives false ideas, pretending to judge of every thing, to ridicule every thing sacred or venerable. These sort of books are all the worse when they are beautifully written, as they generally are; they vitiate the taste, and give a disgust for all healthy food. I knew once a young man in the royal navy whose mind had been completely poisoned by this sort of reading; and when he came to see the evil of it, you cannot think how he spoke to me about these pernicious books. My dearest brother, forgive me for saying all this; but I know your passion for reading, and all I would venture to say is, do not play with poison."

To his favourite sister he added a few words of farewell. She had told him that having, for fun, drawn lots at Christmas as to who should represent the different personages at the Nativity, she had drawn the name of "Mary;" but Théophane's lot had fallen on that of the ass. In reply, Théophane says gaily, "I am very much pleased at the portion awarded me in your drawing. I am to be the ass. Very well. I won't accuse you of a little bit of mischief in the matter, but accept my part. Well, the ass knows how to bray; that is to teach me to be a good trumpeter of the Gospel. The ass receives blows without complaint: may his patience be my model. Again, the poor animal is treated with scorn and derision, his very name is the reverse of a compliment; but he goes on his way just the same. Well, like him, I must disregard human opinion, cultivate humility, bear to be despised, and follow my Lord and Master everywhere, always, and in spite of all. As for you, my darling little sister, you have indeed chosen the better part. Guard it carefully. It is a life of recollection, a life of union with God. I fancy you sitting like Mary at Bethany, at the feet of Jesus, listening to His Word; being gentle, attentive, loving, and caring nothing for the world outside. Your life must be not only the active one of Martha, but the contemplative one of Mary, for both were united in the Mother of our dear Lord. The true science of piety, in fact, consists in reconciling these two. I know you love best to be Mary, but when duty compels you to act as Martha did, do not be *only* Martha, full of anxiety, and 'careful about much serving.' Do the works of Martha with the spirit of Mary; let the interior life leaven the exterior, conforming your will to the Will of Jesus. Dearest sister, imitate Jesus, imitate His holy Mother, and you will be indeed perfect."

CHAPTER VI.

On the 26th of May, 1854, Théophane Vénard, with an older missionary who was returning to Tonquin, said good-bye to the English colony; and as the wind was favourable, a few hours' sail brought them to Macao, where they were most kindly and hospitably entertained by the Spanish Dominicans. M. Vénard, speaking of this town, says, "At the time that the Portuguese were masters of the sea, Macao was an important place. Ships of all nations were anchored in its roadstead, and it was the centre and emporium of all the European commerce with China. The numberless missionaries who have watered the Chinese soil with their blood all started from Macao, from whence they spread themselves to the remotest confines of this great empire. Portugal had a noble mission assigned to her by Providence, but she misunderstood and rejected it. From thence arose her downfall, and it seemed as if God had broken her as one breaks a useless or worn-out instrument. The kings of the earth have never gained any thing in their strifes with the Church of Jesus Christ, and against His vicar on earth, and their victory is magnificently rendered in the Psalms, 'Et nunc, reges, intelligite; erudimini qui judicatis terram.' Macao is indeed a ruin. There is a governor, it is true; but he has no longer any *prestige*. Soldiers still mount guard, but their number is miserably small, and no one has any money to pay them. There are fine houses, but those which are not shut up are occupied by English or Americans. A rich Portuguese scarcely exists; but the poor swarm. The Chinese alone still maintain some kind of trade. Hong Kong gave the death blow to Macao. There are one or two curious things to be seen in the old colony; the tomb of Camoens, buried between two rocks in the midst of the most beautiful scenery, just such as one might imagine should be the grave of a poet. This tomb forms the principal ornament of a garden, which, unfortunately, is ill kept. It is a place much frequented by strangers, and some of them have had the bad taste to cut their names in the rock, and others (among whom, I am sorry to say, are some French sailors) have written stupid and even indecent rhymes on the slab above."

On the 2nd of June our two missionaries left Macao, and we read the following account of their journey in the letters of Théophane to his family:—

"TONQUIN,
"*The Eve of St. John, June* 23, 1854.

"MY DEAREST BROTHERS,—To you I am going to write my first Tonquin letter. I arrived safe and sound at the mission of the Spanish Dominican Fathers, and from thence I take my pen to give you *currente calamo* some details of our voyage. M. Legrand and I embarked at Macao on the 2nd of June, towards evening. We thought our Chinese captain would weigh anchor immediately. Not a bit of it. A Chinaman will never do any thing in a straightforward way. They had to deliberate as to the voyage, consult the Devil, take precautions against pirates, &c. We were to sail in company with other Chinese junks; but the Chinese mistrust one another, and before making an actual start, they feign to go several times, to see if the other ships are ready and trustworthy. Whilst waiting in this way for the real moment of sailing, we went to see a place where the English have a contraband trade in opium. There were we, two poor little European missionaries, among a people who don't admire any thing that comes from Europe, and who are always ready to insult those who do not inspire them with fear. We were thrust into a little hole where we could only sit or lie down, breathing foul air, and covered with vermin. Here we had to stay day and night, for if we attempted to leave it the Chinese called us 'Foreign Devils,' and amused themselves by examining all we had got on, and all that we did. If the departure were delayed, if the wind blew, if we were threatened by pirates, it was we who were to blame. It was impossible to please them. If we tried to be kind to or familiar with them, they despised and insulted us; if we talked little, and maintained a certain gravity and reserve, then we were cold and haughty. The only source of strength and consolation to the missionary in the midst of all these miseries is the cross. With this thought, one passes over many things which would otherwise irritate and wound one; and we can maintain a certain equanimity of character, which is a necessary virtue in the East, but sometimes rather difficult to attain. But I must pass over all such reflections, for the courier is waiting. . . . We set sail at last, in company with seventy other vessels, who had come to an understanding with our captain after much parlying; they were obliged to make a formidable appearance as to numbers in order to intimidate the pirates. We caught sight of six of them in a place called Tin-Pac, and being well armed, fired upon them with the small cannon in our bows: they retreated, and we made all sail towards Haï-Nan, a large island, where we remained several days, anchoring under a town which is said to contain two hundred thousand inhabitants. We did not

dare land, or in fact show ourselves in any way.
One of our missionaries from the diocese of
Poictiers, M. Bisch, is working here, but we could
only salute him with our hearts. On leaving Hai-
Nan, the Chinese junks separated, only a small
number steering for Tonquin. Until then the sea
had been calm and beautiful; afterwards it came on
to blow, and I paid my usual tribute to the fishes
in consequence. . . . Two days later we came in
sight of the shores of Tonquin. I cannot tell you
what I felt as we neared the place of disembarka-
tion. I offered myself again to God, begging Him
to dispose of me as would be most for His glory and
honour, and I invoked my Mother Mary, and my
guardian angel, and the Patron Saints of Tonquin.
. . . . The general view of the country is magnificent; rich plains, with grassy hills, a luxuriant
vegetation, such as one reads of in Robinson Crusoe,
and the whole backed by a magnificent range of
snowy mountains. We entered the harbour by the
mouth of a beautiful river, which glided through
woods and gardens till we cast anchor at a place
called Cuâ Câm, which is the centre of the contraband Chinese trade. It was no longer allowable
for us to see the light of day, and even at night we
only dared to breathe the fresh air on deck with
great precautions. This state of things lasted
(fortunately for us) not more than forty-eight hours.
The mandarin of the Custom House came to inspect
our vessel. We could see this august personage
through the cracks of our prison, scarcely ven-
turing to breathe the while, and most carefully
abstaining from all noise or movement; but the old
fox returned to the shore without having scented
the nest. The next day a Christian boat came for
us, for almost all the inhabitants of Cuâ Câm are
Christians. There was a little misunderstanding

between them and the crew, and for a moment we thought ourselves lost; but we put a good face on it, and the Christian rowers, seeing that we were not afraid, took courage, and brought us in a few hours to the flourishing Mission House of the Spanish Dominicans. Mgr. Hilarion Alcazar received us in his episcopal palace (which, you must understand, is in these countries a simple hut or cabin), and treated us with that generous and delicate hospitality which brings one back in thought to the days of the early Christians. He has insisted on my resting here a few days to recover from the effects of the late voyage, and I am enjoying that ineffable peace and joy which seems to me to be specially sent by our Lord to His missionaries."

M. Vénard continues his recital to his sister a few weeks later as follows:—

"WESTERN MISSION, TONQUIN,
"*Ving Tri*, *July* 31, 1854.

"MY DEAREST SISTER,—You have doubtless read my letter to Henry and Eusebius, describing our voyage from Macao to Tonquin; we heard afterwards that if we had delayed our landing for a few hours only, the news of our death would have followed that of our arrival; for three royal ships, having heard a rumour of our coming, surrounded the Chinese junk in which we had taken our passage, and examined her minutely in every part, as well as other vessels, so that no escape would have been possible. But God preserved us, and at that very moment we were enjoying the refined hospitality of Mgr. Alcazar. We stayed there eight days, but I was ill all the time. An Annamite doctor gave me some fortifying drug or other which enabled me at last to continue my journey. You will wonder at hearing me talk of doctors and medicines, as you probably imagine that I am in a country of savages. But you must know that the civilization of the Annamites equals, if it does not surpass in some points, that of Europe; and they possess physicians of undeniable skill and very high reputations in the country. The one who attended me could tell at once by the pulse the nature of my malady, and said that it arose from derangement of the liver. From Mgr. Alcazar's we went on to Mgr. Hermozilla, a venerable old man, looking like an ancient column left standing amidst the ruins. Nothing can equal the simplicity and piety of this good old bishop. One day, while we were there, the heads of the mission came to him with a complaint that the peasants had not paid up what they call 'the rice of the Blessed Virgin,' a species of tithe for the maintenance of the altars, levied on the congregations, and put under Our Lady's protection. The bishop took the side of the poor, as the rice harvest that month had failed, and finally gained their cause. We stayed only two days at this episcopal palace. Don't let the name mislead you. A bishop's residence here means a poor cabin, half of wood and half of mud, thatched with straw. All the houses are of the same kind, and it is easy to get used to them, for the climate is very hot, and all one wants is protection from the sun and the rain.

"The churches are not more beautiful. A straw roof, sustained by wooden pillars, which are hung with silk on festivals, that is all our splendour. A few rough boards form the altar. If the Annamite Church enjoyed any kind of peace, even for a time, more sumptuous temples would be built. But now it is not worth while to construct any thing but temporary buildings, which may be removed at the breaking out of any fresh persecution. After a few days we started for the Central Vicariate of the Spanish Fathers. We were to have gone by water, but the wind was contrary, and so we were obliged to be transported in a species of net, according to the custom of the country, and in this way to traverse a great number of Pagan villages, and a great market or fair which was being held on the road-side. We were just in the middle of this fair, when we came upon the house of a mandarin, who was the great authority in the place. Now it is a rule that all travellers, unless of superior rank, shall go on foot before these residences, to testify their respect. We did not dare conform to this usage, and show ourselves to the crowd. Our bearers quickened their pace to a trot. Presently came the cry after us, 'Who are those men, who do not get down from their nets?' The catechist, who was the head of our escort, replied that we were 'sick people of his household.' 'At least let them lower their nets,' replied the sentinel. The bearers were compelled to obey. M. Legrand, who knows the language, was in a blue fright. I, on the contrary, who did not in the least understand our danger, thought that we were meant to get out, and with joy began stretching my legs. The bearers, luckily, did not give me the time, but hurriedly raised us again and trotted on. If they had paid us a visit, what a prize they would have found! Soon after we came to the river, and found several Christian junks, into one of which we gladly stepped, and our rowers conveyed us safely to the hut of Mgr. Diaz, Vicar-Apostolic of the Central Mission of Tonquin. Two couriers were waiting for us there, sent by Mgr. Retord to escort us to our final destination.

After a few days' rest we bid good-bye to their cordial, frank, and noble Spanish hospitality, and started on the last stage of our journey, which was not, however, less dangerous. We went in a junk by night, and had to pass by a citadel guarded by 400 soldiers, stationed there to protect a great rice granary belonging to the king. When our boat came opposite the citadel, we were hailed, and asked who we were. The owners of the junk replied that we were mandarins. They did not believe us, and very soon we heard the drum sound the alarm, and a vessel was sent after us in pursuit. Luckily, we had a favourable wind, and being some way ahead, she could not reach us. A second junk followed us, carrying our baggage and attendants. This they attacked, but the men defended themselves bravely, so that they too escaped. This will give you some idea, dearest sister, of the way in which we travel in Tonquin. One goes generally by night, for greater security: sometimes by water, on rivers or canals, with a continual change of boats: sometimes by land, like mighty lords, in palanquins, or on the backs of slaves, in a species of net or hammock, while the matting at the sides hides you from the passers-by. Sometimes one can only go on foot, without shoes, in the little narrow paths between the rice-fields. If it be day-time, one has a fair chance of escaping the difficulties of the road, but at night one must be content to walk 'clumpity-clump,' falling into holes one moment, into rice-water the next, unable to find a firm footing any where; and often, when you think you are going on swimmingly, your foot slips on the greasy damp soil, and you measure your length in the mud. Now don't you think this is a very picturesque way of travelling? I don't say that it is not a little fatiguing now and then, but I assure you it is very laughable at times, and gives rise to a host of comical adventures.

"It was on the 13th of this month that we fairly arrived at the scene of our future labours, that I was introduced for the first time to my Vicar-Apostolic, the illustrious Mgr. Retord, whose name you so often read in the 'Annals.' I found his Grace busy giving a Retreat previous to an Ordination. Mgr. Jeantet, his coadjutor, and Dean of the Tonquin Mission, was helping him. Two other missionaries had also arrived on business. We were therefore six Europeans together—two bishops and four missionaries—a rare event in Tonquin. . . . . You can't think how happy I felt to be one of them; there was such frankness and simplicity—such goodness and condescension on the part of our superiors. Very soon we felt as if we had known each other all our lives, and we talked of every conceivable subject—of France, of Rome, of the Russian war, &c.; and before we separated, we sang together a whole heap of new and old songs and national hymns."

Soon after he wrote to M. Dallet,—
"Who do you think I found here with Mgr. Retord? Who but my dearest friend, F. Theurel, to whom I had wished good-bye with such bitter tears only one short year ago. What is to be said now of *possibilities*, eh! Father Dallet? Here have I been a month in all the delights of Tonquin, for I assure you there are great pleasures here. Theurel preaches, confesses, burns with desire for work; his health is as good as possible. Mine, perhaps, is not first-rate, but what is the use of running? You know the fable, 'Weak health often goes on longest.' So I console myself. Courage! I am always repeating those maxims of St. Theresa's,—

"'Let nothing disturb thee!
Let nothing affright thee!
All passeth away:
　God only shall stay.
Patience wins all.
Who hath God needeth nothing,
For God is his all.'

"I forgot to tell you that all our worldly goods have been pillaged by the Pagans, so that we are destitute of every thing; but what does that signify? He who has God lacks nothing. You will easily believe that my first visit was to the tomb of M. Bonnard. It is close to the altar of the College Chapel."

If M. Vénard was pleased to find his old friend at Tonquin, the joy to M. Theurel was equally great.

"Who would ever have said, or thought, or imagined such good fortune," he exclaimed in a letter to their mutual friend, Father Dallet. "However improbable it may seem, still it is nevertheless a positive fact, that here are Father Vénard and I, *together*, in this western mission of Tonquin, actually in the same village, in the same house, in the same room! To describe the pleasure, the joy it has given us! . . . Yes, but then I feel as if you would break your heart at not being here too. Nevertheless, you must take comfort: *dummodò comprehendam*—that alone is necessary. Will you believe it? Vénard, who has only been here a month, already speaks the language with a perfect accent. I think his little voice is made for it. That's all right. I can only wish you the joy and peace of the poor little Tonquin missionaries."

Théophane's joy at being at last fairly embarked in his work, and in the very mission he would have chosen above all others, found vent in an enthusiastic poem, in which he enlarged on those three great objects of his life: work, the salvation of souls, and death. But before entering upon the way in which he carried out these his three ardent aspirations, we will give a glance at the state of the vineyard to which this fervent labourer was called.

Every one knows that of all the missions in the world those of Cochin-China, the Corea, and Tonquin have been exposed to the cruellest persecutions. Tonquin, perhaps, deserves to be put in the first rank, and therefore it is that the young missionaries look upon it as the grandest of all, and as the vestibule to Heaven. The cross is the programme of all the Tonquin missionaries; for, from the first moment to the last, their lives may be looked upon as one long martyrdom—a martyrdom admirably prefigured by the great cross found on the Aunamite shore by the Dominican missionary, Diego Advarte, in 1596, before any European had set foot in the country.

The Jesuit Fathers were the real founders of the mission, in the person of Father Alexander Rhodes, who died in 1660. From them it passed into the hands of the Paris Foreign Missionary College, to whom it has always proved a ground of singular interest. In fact, from the first missionary martyred in 1684 until the present day, this Infant Church, always under the shadow of persecution, may be said to have grown with her head on the block, and her children's feet steeped in blood.

Still, there have been moments of calm between the storms. The first great persecution was in the eighteenth century, and God avenged it by destroying its authors and depriving them of their thrones. The dynasties of Cochin-China and Tonquin were swept from off the face of the earth, and the rightful heir, replaced by the hand of a Christian Bishop, only resumed his sceptre when he had torn asunder the bloody edicts of the persecutors. Twenty years of peace under this Prince Gia-Long gave breathing time to the Annamite Church, and prepared them for the frightful persecutions of Minh-Menh, that monster in a human form who rivalled Nero in his cruelties. All our readers know, by the "Annals," of the horrible persecution which broke out in 1833 and lasted till 1841. MM. Gagelin, Marchand, Cornay, Jaccard, Borié, with a multitude of Spanish Dominicans and native teachers, fell victims to this relentless tyrant. God did not, however, leave him unpunished; for Minh-Menh was killed by a fall from his horse on the 21st of January, 1841, execrated equally by Pagans and Christians. The new king, Thien-Tri, weary of the bloody edicts of his predecessor, passed an act of amnesty, annulling the penal laws. Unfortunately he died in 1848, and was succeeded by Tu-Duc. During the reign of this prince, famine, cholera, typhus, and other plagues decimated his people; and although these trials enabled the Christians to show themselves in their true colours, and to repay their persecutors by acts of superhuman charity, still the calamities themselves were looked upon as being the result of the Divine vengeance on this new sect, and the mandarins, working on the credulity of the people, fanned the flame of a new persecution, in which, among others, MM. Schoeffler and Bonnard were sacrificed. A temporary peace followed, and it was during that time of comparative security that Théophane had arrived. Nevertheless, in spite of all the obstacles thrown in the way of the preaching of the Gospel, in spite of the small numbers of the Apostolical labourers and the insufficiency of their resources, in spite of this furious persecution of Minh-Menh, which lasted twenty years, there is no country where Christianity has made such wonderful progress as in Tonquin. Mgr. Retord wrote at this very time as follows:—

"When I undertook to govern this mission, sixteen years ago, it did not contain more than a hundred thousand Christians. Now there are 140,000, although the cholera of 1851 carried off 10,000. All these converts, with very few exceptions, practise their religion in a way which would shame many Europeans. They are constant attendants at the Sacraments, and most diligent in the performance of their religious duties. It is useless to add that they are all Catholics. Heretical ministers, with their wives and children, have never attempted to approach these inhospitable and unhealthy shores, or to face a persecution which can only end in one way—martyrdom."

Mgr. Retord was only fifty when M. Vénard arrived at Tonquin. He was still strong and vigorous, in spite of the trials and sufferings he had experienced. He had established a large seminary of native priests, which numbered at that time upwards of seventy-five, all well instructed and full of zeal for the conversion of their countrymen. The College, which he had erected close to his house, had upwards of 200 students, divided into different classes, as in France; while various smaller schools had been established all over the diocese. When the students have finished their College Terms they pass an examination as catechists. Before receiving their diploma, however, they must have converted at least ten Pagans. The theologians are chosen among the catechists; but are only admitted to Holy Orders after a long and vigorous trial. The work of God prospers visibly in this land. In the year 1854 fifteen hundred more souls were added to the Christian ranks. Still the number of Pagans is enormous, if you consider the small area into which they are crowded. But the villages almost touch each other, and are densely populated, while the soil is so fertile that the cost of living is excessively cheap. But to return to Théophane Vénard. Before his arrival in Tonquin, and during his passage, he had had an attack of inflammation of the lungs, which seemed to get worse day by day, in spite of the prescriptions of the Chinese physicians. His entire recovery can only be attributed to a direct Divine interposition, and the account of it will be found in the following letter to his father, written in March, 1855 :—

"When I wrote to you last, my dearest father, I was with Mgr. Retord, at his College of Vinh-Tri. At the end of the month of August, Mgr. sent me to a College, in the village of Kê-Doan to study the Annamite language, and associated with me two catechists who could speak a little Latin. I passed by Kénon, which is the great seminary directed by Mgr. Jeantet, Mgr. Retord's coadjutor. I stayed there for eight days. Mgr. Jeantet is sixty-three years old, and has been thirty-seven years in the mission. He is a most venerable old man, and also most kind and amiable. He was never tired of asking me questions about France, that country so dear to the missionary's heart. I was also very much interested in seeing the seminary, and began stammering out some words of Annamite which I had just learnt. Then I started, as I have said before, for the College of Lâng-Doân. A month in such a study as this went like lightning. On the second Sunday in October I ventured to preach a short sermon in the little church. The chiefs of the village came to congratulate me, not that I believe they could understand much of my allocution, but that being Annamites, they are very civil and courteous; and though I had made such a hash of their language, they thought it right to compliment me.

"Some days after I fell sick of a pestilential illness, which declared itself in the College, and I was one of its first victims. My catechists nursed me with great care and attention, and Mgr. Retord, Mgr. Jeantet, and M. Castex, Pro-Vicar-General of the mission, sent me all sorts of medicines, which, with the grace of God, cured me. As soon as I could stand I went for change of air in a boat to another village named Kè-Dâm, where an Annamite priest has his principal residence. Be it observed, that I went in a boat *across the fields*, because every year at this time there is an inundation caused by the overflowing of the rivers, the result of the tropical rains in the mountains to the west. Then the whole country becomes like one vast sea. The villages themselves are all under water, and the only means of communication is by boats. I found myself well enough on All Saints' Day to say a low Mass. The evening before all the village gathered round the church, to congratulate me on my recovery. The chiefs, dressed in their best clothes, came to conduct me solemnly to church, to the sound of native music and repeated hurrahs. You see, dearest father, that the Annamites care for their missionaries. But the evening of the Feast of All Saints was the reverse of the medal. I was hardly gone to bed, when they came to wake me, and to announce the arrival of a mandarin for a domiciliary visit. They were in a great fright, and implored me to go on to another village. Though the news was not very certain, I thought I had better comply with their wishes, and so packed up my traps as fast as I could. I was carried with all my little establishment on men's backs in the middle of the night to the said village. This was my first nocturnal flight; since then I have had many others! I remained eight days in the house of a devout Christian in this place, who seemed as if he could not make enough of me; and to show him my gratitude I made a great distribution of medals and chaplets amongst them all. Then I went on to a College situated in the little town of Hoàng-Nguyên, where M. Castex has his principal residence. M. Castex was on a diocesan tour, and was not to return till the month of December. I was, therefore, the only European in the College, at the head of which was a native priest, an Annamite father. Here I first began to hear confessions, first of the students, and then of the Christians of the village; but I made little or no progress, because very soon I fell sick again of an inflammation of the lungs, which endangered my life. But after a time I recovered. M. Castex returned with M. Titaud, and then came another of our missionaries, M. Néron, so that we were four altogether. You can fancy what a pleasure it was! After some days of mutual enjoyment, M. Titaud returned to his district. M. Néron also prepared to go back to his College of Vinh-Tri, of which he is the superior; but he was taken prisoner in crossing the river, and very nearly gave us a fresh martyr. By a special providence, the soldier, who had hastened to the village to get a reinforcement in order to secure our poor brother, met the Chief of the Canton, who knew and had a great regard for him; so although a Pagan he connived at his escape, and the only loss was a certain sum of money.

"You will want to know more about my health. On New Year's day I was so ill that I could hardly receive the visits of congratulation of the Christians of the district. The bishop sent me his own physician, a very clever man, whose medicines did me some good, but after his departure I fell sick again. M. Castex took every possible care of me, and was extremely anxious and troubled on my account. I was obliged to give up confessing, or saying Mass, or office, or even reading and writing, and I was scarcely allowed to speak at all. At last M. Castex advised me to make a Novena to the Sacred Hearts of Jesus and Mary, and insisted on sharing it with me. We began it on the day of the Purification, and at once I felt myself getting better, and since that all bad symptoms have disappeared, and my strength is nearly returned. To the Sacred Hearts of Jesus, Mary, and Joseph be the praise.

"About this time the political horizon darkened: a revolutionary party broke out in Tonquin; a new edict, emanating from the king, denounced our holy religion; evil-disposed persons betrayed the residences of the missionaries to the mandarins; the College of Kê-Vinh was dispersed; and Monseigneur Retord, with several of his missionaries, had to keep themselves in hiding. The mandarin of Kê-Cho, the capital of Tonquin, laid siege to the great Seminary of Kê-Non, but Mgr. Jeantet had already taken flight to the mountains, from whence he wrote to M. Castex and me, 'I have been looking up my old haunts, and the caves where I lived at the time of the persecution of Minh-Menh, not that it is very easy for an old man like me to scramble up and down rocks and precipices. I sometimes wonder how I manage to get on at all.' The mandarin only found an Annamite father and a deacon, whom he released soon after, although not without the payment of 10,000 francs, but at least the College of Kê-Non is still standing.

"As for M. Castex and I, after having been chased from one village to the other, we have finally taken refuge in a female convent near the town of Bùt-Dông, where we have lived as hermits with two catechists for the last two months. Very soon, however, I hope we shall be able to show our faces again, as the storm seems to have cooled down. Nevertheless we must be prudent, for the denouncer of Mgr. Jeantet, having failed to catch him, has offered his own head to the mandarin if he cannot deliver a European before the end of the year into his hands. Every one, therefore, keeps himself on his guard. What will happen, God knows; in any case it is better to hope than to fear, and, as Mgr. Retord writes to us, 'Jesus and Mary will not abandon us now more than they have done before. Pray then with great confidence, and do not let us be discouraged or give way to sadness. If any of us win the martyr's palm, so much the better. *Sicut fuerit voluntas tua, sic fiat.*'

"The rebellion goes on spreading: it wants to re-establish the ancient dynasty on the throne, and they say that they will soon present the new king. On the other hand the misery is very great. Last year's rice harvest was bad; this year it is simply lost in many places: thousands of people are dying of hunger. It is enough to move any one to compassion. People in Europe have no idea what the public misery is of this unhappy country. The feasts for the new year, which generally are so gay, have passed this season in sadness and mourning, and it is not probable that the end of the year will be brighter. Now, dearest father, I must stop. À Dieu. Do not be anxious about me. *What God keeps is well kept.* Keep well; pray for me; and may the joy of our Lord Jesus Christ fill your heart for evermore."

The missionary had not said much in this letter of his relations with the people. He filled up that void in the following letter to his sister:—

"You say you would wish to be a little bird, my dearest sister, and see how I get on with my new children. Well, I assure you I begin to love them very much. The Annamite people are thoroughly good, and their respect for the missionaries is very great. Until now the state of the country, and my small acquaintance with their language, has prevented my doing much, but, nevertheless, the principal people of the villages often come to see me, and to bring me some little present. I could only say a few unintelligible sentences at first, which I saw made them very much inclined to laugh, but they would not have done so for all the world, so afraid are they of hurting my feelings. Very often, too, the peasants come and pay me a visit: one day it is the father of a family, who has married one of his children, and comes to bring me a pig's head killed for the feast; another day some poor mother arrives to recommend her son who is just starting for the army; another time four or five poor women club together to offer me a little basket of fruit, or to ask me for a chaplet or a cross. I could only answer them in a few words, but every one went away pleased and satisfied. It is the custom among the Annamites for no one to present himself to a superior without offering a present. But, besides that, if our poor Christians ever have any fine fruit, or fine fish, or any vegetable larger than usual, they have the greatest delight in coming to offer it to the missionaries. I assure you, Mélanie, I love the Annamites very much, and I thank God every day that He has consecrated me to their service. All is not, certainly, *couleur de rose*; but there will always be thorns in every path.

"One word, besides, as to the Tonquinese nuns, about whom you make such eager inquiries. They are natives living in community under the authority of an abbess; but they do not take vows, so that they are received very young. They work in the fields, or prepare the cotton for linen cloths, or else go and *sell pills*, which will astonish you, and probably make you laugh; but it is by this means that they can gain access to sick Pagan children, and baptize those who are in danger of death.

"They live hardly and poorly, pray a great deal, give themselves the discipline, and fast far more than the run of ordinary Christians. When necessary they act as couriers to carry the letters from one mission to another, in which they are often invaluable; and there is nothing in this occupation which shocks the feelings or customs of their country. On such occasions they always go in twos. They are the couriers of the different missions, often bearing immense weights; but they are accustomed to toil and fatigue, as all Annamite women are. The Christians call them always '*Sisters*,' and they are universally loved and respected.

"It is a very agreeable thing to hear the Tonquinese prayers, especially when they go well together; it is a harmony which has often touched me more than the most beautiful European music. They have some very pretty litanies of Our Lady, especially one of the Immaculate Conception. But their acts of thanksgiving after communion are the most touching; when I hear them, it moves me almost to tears. The Annamites do not know how to pray to themselves, or in a low voice; and even if there be only one communicant, they intone their thanksgiving out loud, either alone or in company with the choir. The catechists sing the plain chant very well, and sometimes sing the High Mass; but then there is always a musical accompaniment. Their instruments are the violin, the harp, drums, fife, and cymbals. They have not much variety in their music, and during High Mass will play one tune from beginning to end till one is satiated with it. But after all, God, perhaps, is as much praised and glorified by this simple, devout congregational music as by the most magnificent harmony, executed by first-rate artists. It is the vibration of the heart, and not of the chords, which is acceptable to Him.

"And my Latin scholars, you ask, are they very learned? It is rather difficult that they should be, not having any dictionaries. At the end of their studies they understand the Catechism of the Council of Trent, and of late years Mgr. Retord has started a class of philosophy, which they do in Latin. You may well imagine that we do not trouble our heads to teach Ovid, Horace, or heathen mythology, to these poor Tonquinese, so that the controversy as to the classics must be judged by itself."

In a letter to an old friend about this time we find a touching passage showing the simplicity and *naïveté* of these poor people in their religious rites:—

"I am quite sure that the first marriage ceremony you performed was widely different from mine. In Tonquin there is no marriage procession or bridesmaids, as there is in France. They receive the Sacrament as they do the Blessed Eucharist, and without any further demonstration. Well, my *fiancés* having been to confession, and prepared themselves in that way for the Sacrament of Marriage, the day was fixed, and I went very early in the morning, and

sang Mass to the whole population, for they keep
early hours in Tonquin. Then my catechist signed
to the young couple (each about eighteen years of
age) to go up to the altar. The young girl mounted
the steps; but where was her betrothed? He
never appeared. After waiting for some time in
vain, the poor child was quietly told to go back,
and to come again at the same time to-morrow.
Resigned and gentle, she obeyed. The next day
the future husband duly made his appearance at
the proper moment, and I blessed the marriage.
In the course of the day the young couple, con-
ducted by the sister of the bride, came to pay me
a visit, and to thank me. I ventured to ask why
the young gentleman had not made his appearance
the first day? He answered, with perfect simplicity, that 'he had not woke in time to come to
church!'"

We think we cannot better describe both the
people themselves and the life of the young and
fervent missionary, than by continuing to transcribe
his letters, which are such graphic pictures of his
daily trials and their consolations. In September,
1855, he writes again to his family,—

"I hope that my last letters, written in March,
have reached you? Since then, it has pleased
God to throw me again on a bed of sickness. On
Ash-Wednesday I went to M. Castex, Vicar-General
of the mission, who was at the College of Hoàng-
Nguyên. The road was not more than a quarter of
a league, but the road was full of mud and water.
I took a violent chill, being first hot and then cold;
and from that moment I got worse and worse. I
had likewise to fly by night several times from the
mandarins, and hide in the rice-fields, which did
not mend matters. The people around me thought
that the end was at hand, and prepared every thing

for my funeral. But then God sent me a doctor, who gave me some new sort of medicine, which brought me to life again. I received Extreme Unction twice, and each time God was pleased, in strengthening my soul, to restore my body. I am now staying at Kê-Vinh with Mgr. Retord, who hopes thereby to complete my cure; but I am afraid it will be difficult, as my left lung is almost gone. I have terrible perspirations and oppression on my chest; and in the morning I sometimes have such violent expectoration and running at the nose, that I cannot say Mass. On the other hand, my appetite is good, so that I am able to go on with my little studies. Do not let my illness make you unhappy, my dearly-loved people! but pray for me, that the sufferings of my body may be for the spiritual welfare of my soul. . . . ."

A little later, he writes,—

"I am dying out like a candle, and hold to life by a mere thread. I think the doctors have given me up; but I can still rejoice in whatever God appoints. Perhaps this is the last note you will receive from me. Pray for me, that though my poor body perishes from day to day, my soul may be saved through His merits Who died for me. We shall meet one another in a brighter and better home. À Dieu!"

To resume the September letter,—

"The persecution threatened to be terrible; but, thank God! it has not realized our worst apprehensions. Our purses have suffered most; for one could only close the mandarins' mouths by bars of silver. Our poor missions have indeed been bled to satisfy Pagan rapacity. These poor Annamites are always the victims of some misfortune or act of oppression. One year comes an inundation; the next, a drought. The harvest almost always fails. A bowl of rice is all that these poor people wish for, and even that they cannot always obtain. Yet these rapacious gentlemen, the mandarins, who are nominally their fathers and protectors, think of nothing but pillage and robbery, and suck the wealth out of these unhappy people like so many leeches. I really do not believe there is such a thing as an honest man among the mandarins. The Christians are a capital bank for them; for their religion, being proscribed by the king, it is the easiest thing in the world to accuse them at any moment of 'treason and rebellion against the state.' From the village mayors up to the mandarin governors of the provinces, every single man will have his share in the plunder. In a village which is half Christian and half Pagan, the Christians pay a heavy ransom to have liberty of conscience. . . . . . This year we have had no martyrdom. I have only heard of a doctor and his two brothers, who were thrown into prison by the mandarin, and are still in captivity. I know this physician; he is a most fervent and excellent man, who has already been a Confessor for the Faith in the Minh-Menh persecution. Thanks to the interposition of a friendly mandarin at court, Mgr. Retord has been able to return to his College; and Mgr. Jeantet is likewise gone back to his great seminary. So after the storm comes the calm, and God protects His own. Since the month of January I have not had a line from any of you, and am getting rather anxious for tidings. May God and His Holy Mother preserve you, my dearest father, and sister, and brothers, from all evil, now and for evermore!"

On the 1st of December, he wrote again to his sister, saying that he had recovered his strength; that his left side was much better; and that she must join with him in thanking and praising God for having so unexpectedly restored him to health. He continues,—

"We have got a period of comparative peace; so that our schools are reopened. The bishop can officiate pontifically on festivals; and we may go, *in the daytime*, to walk in the College gardens—a favour of which you would understand the magnitude better if you had been confined, like us, for so long a time in one room without daring either to sing or speak above a whisper. Lately the Government has been put in a state of excitement by the appearance of an English man-of-war at Touranne, which is close to the capital of the kingdom in Cochin-China. I believe that the Governor-General of Hong Kong and the Plenipotentiaries of Queen Victoria came to propose a treaty of commerce to Tu-Duc, the Annamite king. However, this 'gracious sovereign' would not receive the despatches; so that the English had to retire without doing any thing. But the consequences have been rather disastrous for us, as they choose to fancy we sent for them. All this time we have had no news from home for more than a year. I try to be patient, but each courier who arrives and brings no letters is a fresh mortification. Pray for me, that I may strive to live above all these feelings, and become a more worthy priest of Jesus Christ; so that in the difficult post which I now occupy, I may have the necessary grace and prudence. As for me, I never cease to pray for you all. Remember your poor little Théophane!"

At this time the Crimean war and the proclamation of the dogma of the Immaculate Conception occupied the minds of men in Europe, of every class. Although sixteen months had elapsed since he had had any letters from home, yet the news of these two great events reached our missionaries, and rejoiced their sad hearts. Théophane wrote to express his joy to his sister, and adds,—

"Since my last letter, the persecution has been renewed, and one of our native priests, Huông, has been martyred. That did not prevent Mgr. Retord from preaching his Lenten missions, and, thanks to Our Lady's protection, we have not had to take many more precautions than usual. As far as I am concerned, I had the pleasure of accompanying his Grace in one of his diocesan tours, where the work was arduous and incessant. He celebrated the Offices of Holy Week and Easter at Kê-Vinh to an immense congregation, and the whole passed off well, and in comparative peace, if such a word can be applied to people in our position. You will perhaps wonder how, being continually on the '*qui vive*,' and in hiding, and a price being put upon our heads, we can think of keeping feasts and talk of peace. But it seems as if a special protection of God and of the Blessed Virgin rested upon us, so that we may 'serve Him without fear.' Besides, when we do get a little liberty, you must set it against the continual vexations and constraints to which we are generally subject. We are like rats coming out for a little bit, regardless of the cat, and hastening to regain our holes on the first alarm or sound of danger."

At last, after nineteen months' fast, the poor missionaries received their home letters. After answering them in detail, Théophane continues,—

"On the Feast of St. Peter, Mgr. Retord convoked all his missionaries and his coadjutor, Mgr. Jeantet, to meet him at the College of Kê-Vinh. We made a Retreat in common, and then passed fifteen days of the most perfect calm and peace, in spite of the emissaries of the mandarins who were spying in the neighbourhood. We sang heaps of French songs, and enjoyed ourselves thoroughly. Just before we parted, arrived a courier from Cochin-China, bringing us news of the success of the allies, the proclamation of peace, the birth of the Prince Imperial, and the rejoicings of the people at the new dogma. In addition to all this we were told of the mission sent by the Emperor to negotiate with the Annamite king, so as to stop the persecution of the Christians, and especially of the French missionaries, whose blood their king, a worthy successor of his father, has so cruelly shed. We were about to disperse to our respective missions, and we had already taken leave of one another, when there came on a tremendous inundation, worse than any that had been known in the memory of the oldest inhabitant, and compelled us to stay where we were. The flood lasted a whole month, and the waters covered four large provinces, besides breaking down the dykes in a great many places. The newly-sown rice was completely lost; that which was almost ready for the harvest was submerged, and the great portion rotted; a great many villages have been destroyed, and thousands of persons have been drowned, or killed by the falling of the mud walls of their houses. Many took refuge in the mountains; others huddled close to the dykes which had resisted the rush of waters, and remained there without food for days; others, again, were like ourselves kept close prisoners to their houses, having to battle with the ever-rising flood. Often it was necessary to take up the flooring, and make a temporary standing-ground in the upper story, or close under the roof, which had to be pierced to give air. In the villages where inundations are an annual occurrence, they have a system of boats, which are kept ready in case of need, but in other places you can imagine the misery! Besides that, their gardens are all destroyed, their trees killed, and their cattle and domestic animals drowned. As for ourselves, the students of the College, by dint of working day and night, contrived to build a dyke sufficiently strong to protect the church and the place where we had taken refuge, but the bishop's house was full of water. In the midst of this I fell sick of a violent fever, with an attack of asthma, and it was in one of the worst fits that your letter was brought to me, and acted like the dew on the parched ground. Don't fancy that this is a figure of speech. I do assure you it is a fact that the sight of your handwriting, and the joy that I felt, reacted upon my whole system, and the fever was sensibly diminished. However, just as I was beginning to rejoice in a kind of convalescence, I caught the typhoid fever, which again brought me to the very gates of death. Mgr. Retord and my fellow-missionaries said Masses for me to St. Peter of Alcantara, to whom, St. Theresa says, our Lord refuses nothing, and I got better from that time. The end of all this succession of fevers is, that although I am about again, I am still very weak; but as my appetite has returned, I hope soon to be able to work. My left side no longer gives me so much pain; and as God has preserved me until now, so I hope that He will do so to the end, and enable me to do something for His glory before I die."

After receiving these letters, his family naturally feared that the following courier would bring the news of his death. Their surprise and joy were therefore very great at the contents of a letter, dated June, 1857, in which he says, "At the end of the year 1856 every one thought me dying, and so I took

K

the advice of Mgr. Retord, and consented to try a Chinese remedy, which is only used in extreme cases, and which is called, in the Annamite tongue, '*Phep-Quênou.*' In Europe it would be considered a species of cauterization. It consists in burning little balls of a certain herb, rather like absinth, on different parts of the body. There are, the Chinese doctors say, 360 points in the human body which may be thus burnt. The difficulty is to know which is the right spot; as, otherwise, you may be lamed, or become blind, or have your mouth drawn on one side, &c., &c. Having submitted to this operation, they burnt me in 500 different places, about 200 of which were near and round the lungs. At the end of a few days these cauterizations, or inoculations, produced a little yellow pustule full of matter; that is a sign that the operation has been successful, as the system is supposed in this way to reject all that is noxious. The result has been that I am wonderfully better, and so my patience in enduring this small purgatory for several hours has been rewarded. But enough of my wretched ailings, for to be sick is natural to me; and Mgr. Retord declares I have chosen sufferings in my speciality! I would rather talk to you about the state of our poor mission. We were at Kê-Vinh in February, when one Monday, at eight o'clock, one of the villagers came in hot haste to tell us that the mandarin of the southern province had surrounded the village, and was coming to seize us. Mgr. Retord was forced by the students into a subterranean hiding-place; M. Charbonnier and I were stuffed into a place between two walls, where we remained for four hours without seeing the light of day. At the end of that time, they came to announce to us that the domiciliary visit was over, and the mandarin gone!

but that he had carried off with him the director of the College, a venerable priest named Tinh, one of his catechists, and the mayor of the place. The truth was, that in the neighbouring province certain Christians had been forced by blows to reveal the bishop's residence; and a poor woman, who was the bearer of some European letters to one of our missionaries, was seized, put to the torture, and confessed in her agony, that they were destined for the College of Kê-Vinh. But this was only the beginning of a series of misfortunes. In March the mandarin returned with 200 soldiers to destroy both the Church and College; but we had received warning in time, and had all taken refuge in the mountains. The next day we returned to find every thing in ruins, and as we were surrounded by spies, it was thought better to leave the place for a time. I went by night, secretly in a boat, to my old quarters of Hoàng-Nghuyên, while Mgr. Retord and M. Charbonnier returned to their hiding-places in the mountains. M. Castex and M. Theurel, the superior of the College, were at Hoàng when I arrived; but the former was soon seized with rheumatic fever, and became dangerously ill. Mgr. Retord, hearing of this, came down from the hills to administer the last consolations to our dear friend and brother, who expired on the eve of the Feast of the Holy Trinity, after great sufferings. His death was, however, perfectly peaceful, and he slept the sleep of the just. To me, who had lived in great intimacy with him for two years, the loss is very great, and I have scarcely courage to face the future. Mgr. Retord has given me his post, for which I feel utterly unworthy. May I only imitate the holiness of my predecessor, and win as many souls for our dear Master! Our good old priest Tinh, of whom I spoke as having been carried off by the persecutor, made a glorious confession of faith, and was instantly beheaded, without the Christians having time to prepare any thing to help him in his last moments. But he was one who kept his lamp ever burning. The sword of the executioner broke in half during the operation, which the mandarins thought a bad omen, and in consequence offered up pagan sacrifices to appease the manes of the victim. Poor Tinh's three companions, having also generously confessed the faith, were condemned to perpetual banishment to a distant and unhealthy mountain. A few months later, a pagan prefect, having taken a spite against Mgr. Diaz, a Dominican bishop, denounced him to the mandarins, and his Grace was seized at his residence in the village of Biù-Chu, and dragged to the prefecture, where he is imprisoned and vigorously guarded. We expect every day to hear that he has been condemned to death. The great mandarin has taken a special hatred to all Christians just now, and has placed crosses at all the gates of the town, so that every one in going out or coming in may trample it under their feet! The unhappy Christians were subject to domiciliary visits day and night. Fortunately, however, they were warned in time, and the greater number have taken flight. In Cochin-China the state of things is still worse. I told you, in a previous letter, that the Emperor was going to send a plenipotentiary to plead the cause of the Christians with the Annamites. Well, M. de Montigny duly arrived, but only with two little steamers and a corvette, and with no real powers to treat. So the king refused to listen to them, and the Frenchmen had to weigh anchor and go; and all the people, whether Christians or pagans, who had been rejoicing at the prospect of being delivered from their tyrants, seeing the failure of the whole thing, were not only thoroughly discouraged, but began to despise a power which could do nothing, and this shame has fallen heavily on us poor missionaries. If France meddles at all, she ought to do it thoroughly, so as to carry her point. Still, all hope is not gone, as the Chinese war has brought so large a fleet into these waters. M. de Montigny, unable to help us as he wished, threatened the king with the account he would have to render to our ships of the French blood shed in his dominions. The king, seeing the interest he took in the Christian missionaries, imagined that he had been sent for by them; therefore, when he set sail and went away, he left us in the claws of a tiger who was more and more irritated against us. In consequence, they seized a Christian mandarin with thirty of his neophytes, and after having made them suffer horrible tortures, they were condemned to be beheaded. Then the poor mandarin was dragged through all the streets of the capital, and at each corner his sentence was read out, and he received thirty blows with a stick. This sentence was full of blasphemies against our Lord; saying, 'The Christians pretend that those who suffer such tortures are sure of Paradise after their death. Who knows that? Fools that they are! If it were so, why does not their Jesus come and deliver them?' Oh, my Lord! Thou hast heard their words, and wilt remember them. Yes, I have a firm conviction that Thou wilt succour us and avenge Thy name!"

After the death of M. Castex, as we have said before, F. Vénard remained at the College of Hoàng-Nghuyên, where he had the joy of being once more with his great friend, M. Theurel. But the difficulty of carrying on the work of the missions, owing to the violence of the persecution, weighed heavily on his mind. "I sometimes ask myself," he writes, "Is God's grace no longer so effective as before? Is the time passed for the conversion of the Gentiles? Or are we poor missionaries less zealous than our predecessors? It is quite heartbreaking to look around one, and to see nothing but heathen pagodas, to hear nothing but the bells of the bonzes, to see nothing but diabolical processions! Our dear Lord has to bow before the ministers of Buddha and Confucius. His missionaries live in holes and caverns, and a price is put upon their heads. Is not the day of their deliverance at hand? In this Annamite kingdom the penal laws are most cruel and rigid, but they are only half carried out, on account of the greed of the mandarins, who simply use them as a means to extort money. If at least one might buy peace with the money! But no; this half and half persecution undoes every thing. One day you build a church, open a school, establish a college. The next week perhaps you have to fly, and your works are all destroyed. At another time you pay a large sum to a mandarin to be left in peace. Then he goes out of office, and another one comes, who perhaps asks double the price, which it is impossible to raise; and then the edifice you have raised with such pains and labour crumbles away! As for me, I have no hope but in God and in His immaculate Mother, whose conception has just been so gloriously proclaimed. Under the yoke of the oppressor, we are like the Jewish captives, '*Super flumina Babylonis.*' But I look on this proclamation as a rainbow, which is to announce to us the end of the storm."

In September, 1857, he wrote again to his sister,—

"MY DEAREST SISTER,—You will have seen by my last letter that my health was improved, and that Mgr. Retord had given me a new district. I have upwards of twelve thousand Christians here, divided into four large parishes, with six or seven native priests under me. My duty is to go from parish to parish, seeing that all is in good order; establish peace if there should be discord; give the necessary dispensations; confirm, in cases where the Bishop or Vicar-Apostolic cannot come to perform that sacramental function; give retreats and missions; in fact, strive to augment in all hearts the love of God and the zeal for His Church. As to the Pagans, I have never counted them, but there must be from 250,000 to 300,000. It needs ten St. Francis Xaviers to bring all these people to the knowledge of the Gospel. At this moment it is difficult for us to do much in the way of conversions, on account of the virulence of the persecution. But still from time to time a certain number of souls are garnered in. When the children are ill, the mothers bring them for baptism. The other day a young widow brought me her little one who was dying. She herself was in the greatest misery, having eaten only five times in twelve days. I baptized her child, and then entrusted her to the care of one of our Christian women, who is preparing her likewise for that holy sacrament. After the Feast of the Assumption I went to a district which was almost entirely Pagan. Only about two hundred Christians were scattered here and there. It was close to the residence of the mandarin. No European had ever penetrated so far into the interior; so I had to keep myself as secret as I possibly could. But the children whom I had confirmed betrayed me unintentionally, by chattering, and saying, that ' there was a little European come into the village, very small, but very white and pretty;' for you must know, my dear little sister that we poor Europeans pass for great beauties, and that one who is considered dark in France appears white among these people, who are burnt a mahogany colour by a tropical sun. Well, what was to be done? The hare was started, and the dogs on the scent! I resolved not to lose courage; but putting my whole trust in God, I worked day and night in this His neglected vineyard during one whole week; while the Christians, who were in a terrible fright, acted as sentinels, and refused all visitors whose curiosity prompted them to wish to have a look at the European. Having finished my work, I departed secretly by night, favoured by the darkness, and came to another place, where the villagers, amounting to 4000 or 5000 souls, were all Christians, and the neighbourhood, though pagan, was favourable to Christianity. My goings and comings are easy at this season of the year, as the inundations last for four or five months. The country becomes an immense sea, in which float green villages. There are no roads. Every one goes in boats; but fortunately there are plenty of these of all shapes and sizes. I have got one which just holds one person, very light, woven of bamboo; and every evening, I, sitting like a tailor in my little skiff, paddle myself along to my different penitents, often meeting one or the other on the way, and then having races which shall row the quickest, in which manœuvre I need not say your poor brother is always beaten. I make a point of visiting my flock in their own homes, which gives them immense pleasure. In fact, it is impossible to find a better-disposed people than these poor Annamites, or to meet more fervent or pious souls. This year and the last the inundations have been extraordinary, and above a foot of water came into my house. I had fishes, frogs and toads, crabs and serpents, swimming about my room very happily, I being perched on some planks about three or four inches only above them. But what I disliked most was that the rats insisted on taking refuge on my mat, and one night I squashed one while I was asleep. It was a disagreeable discovery, but I was very thankful afterwards, as, on waking, I found a venomous viper, striped black and white, who had likewise coiled itself up on my poor bed, as if to ask for hospitality, and who was hissing just when I stretched out my toes. So I forgave the rat. However, I determined, under the circumstances, to raise my house. I got the Christians to bring me a quantity of earth, and then lift up my house four or five feet. For you must know that this house, like all the rest, consists only of two or three wooden columns, interlaced with bamboo trellice, outside which is a thin plaster of mud, which is again covered with a coating of lime, that is, when it is wanted to look grand. The height is never more than ten or fifteen feet, and the roof is made of dry leaves. All this edifice is therefore easy enough to transport, as it is very light, and a man can lift it in his hand. So now I am high and dry, and out of the way of the water. I have actually made a little garden, with flower seeds from Europe, and have got a rose tree, a honeysuckle, some balsams, and some stocks. Don't you think that was very persevering? But now, my darling little Mélanie, don't you go and imagine, in your foolish, loving sister's heart, that I am a great saint. I am not even a little wee one! Sickness has weakened my poor body, and stupefied my senses, and cooled my ardour. You see I own all my spiritual miseries to you, so that you may both pity and pray for me. My heart is as cold and icy sometimes as the tropical sun is burning and hot. There are no beautiful churches or services here to rouse one's tepidity, and drop a little dew of piety on one's frigid soul. Pray then for me, dearest sister, that the heavenly dew may descend and soften your brother's heart; that his interior life may be strengthened, and his prayers become more fervent, and the spirit of sacrifice more entire; so that he who bears the grand title of missionary may do works worthy of the name. Ask also that God may give me a little more health and strength, for you know how the body reacts on the soul; and if the labourer stumbles in tracing the furrow, it will be crooked and only half done. Beg the Author of All Good for these gifts which I so greatly need, so that His work may be better done, and His name be glorified.

"You ask me if I should not like some object of devotion, or something for my church. If you could manage to make me a chasuble I should be most grateful, and my catechists would be delighted. Only yesterday they said to me, 'Oh, father, do write to France, and get a prettier set of vestments for Mass on Feast Days.'

"And now, dearest sister, God bless and keep you and all near and dear to us. I recommend myself specially to the prayers of all who care for your unworthy brother, THÉOPHANE."

CHAPTER VII.

THE letters written by Pére Vénard in May, 1858, did not reach their destination, so to fill up the gap in the account of the events which preceded his martyrdom, we must have recourse to the report of Mgr. Retord.

"Our position," he writes, "is terrible at this moment. We are like birds on the branch of a tree, always on the alert, always receiving messages to say that we have been discovered by the spies, that we have been denounced, that the mandarins are surrounding our mission, and that such and such Christians have been pillaged, tortured, and put to death on our account. To try and spare them, we hide either in our little boats, or in caverns, or in tombs in the mountains, where we run the risk of being buried alive. One day we had to remain in one of these for eight hours, being only able to breathe through a bamboo tube. When we came out we were all like idiots, and only half conscious. But the corporal pains we endure are nothing to the anguish of our souls, lest any of our neophytes should deny their faith under the torture. The researches of the mandarins are so active, that it is almost impossible to escape them. One of our native priests was seized last week, and thrown into prison, from which he was only released by martyrdom. His companions and scholars, who had been arrested at the same time, were condemned to a perpetual exile, and amongst them was a little child of ten years old who, rather than renounce Jesus Christ, bore the strokes of the bastinadoe, and the separation from his parents and his home, and to wear till death the malefactor's chain. Another priest and a catechist were apprehended the next day, and gained the martyr's palm. Two new edicts against us have been fulminated, which have greatly kindled the zeal and fury of our Pagan governors. Our chapels are destroyed, our houses demolished, our schools dispersed, and our money wasted in vain attempts to buy off our converts. There is not one of my poor missionaries who has not his personal troubles besides. MM. Theurel and Vénard, surrounded by their trembling, weeping flock, have been obliged to take refuge in some subterranean caverns, where the mandarins as yet have been unable to follow them. M. Titaud saw his church and house destroyed before his eyes, and hid himself with difficulty in a wild solitude, exposed to the attacks of all kinds of venomous creatures. The same thing has happened to M. Saiget. M. Mathevon, hard pressed, nearly fell into the hands of the enemy, who had already seized his catechist and his guide, when it suddenly occurred to him to throw himself between two or three old mats, and he thus escaped detection. Mgr. Jeantet has been obliged to stop his theological class, and take refuge in the mountains; God knows when he will be able to return to his post. Even M. Charbonnier and I, who hoped to have escaped the storm in my little retreat of Vinh-Tri, have had to seek the shelter which men denied us of the bears and tigers who have their holes in the rocks. MM. Galy and Néron, who are at the extremity of the mission, have enjoyed a certain immunity until now, but I expect every day to hear of fresh disasters."

Then follows a recital of the tortures to which the poor Christians are exposed, to try and compel them to apostatize, of which we will give a *résumé* here, that people at home may know what it is which is borne at this very hour by men and women like ourselves, in those distant countries, for the name and for the love of our Lord and Master Jesus Christ.

The most ordinary torture is the "cangue." It

is a species of ladder, four or five feet long, and varying in weight from ten pounds to forty pounds, of which the two sides are united at a width of six inches by four iron bars. The head of the martyr is passed through the middle bars, and the two heavy sides rest on the shoulder. To bear this day and night is perfect misery. The neck and shoulders become quite raw; and when their inhuman jailers drag them in this way from side to side, the agony may be imagined.

In the prison itself, which is a species of hell upon earth, a fresh torture is resorted to. This is a kind of stocks, in which the feet are caught just above the ancle; very often these are too tight, and enter the flesh, for which there is no remedy. What makes it more insupportable is the fact that innumerable bugs live in the cracks of the wood, and suck the blood of the victims all the while. These stocks being immovable, the unhappy prisoners are obliged to remain in the same position day and night, either sitting or crouching, without being able to move in the least.

The third torture, and one universally employed, is the "rotin" or knout, which is inflicted in the most brutal manner. The victims are laid flat on their stomachs in long rows, one after the other, the feet of the one being fastened to the hands of the next, and all so stretched out as almost to dislocate their joints. Each blow inflicted produces blood, and gives an involuntary start to the whole, like an electric shock, so that those who are not struck suffer nearly as much as those who are; and as they leave a certain interval between each stroke, the torment lasts several hours, as each sufferer receives fifty or sixty blows. The instrument used for this horrible flagellation is a flexible whip, about the size of a little finger, and about four feet long. The lash is split into four bits, which are afterwards firmly tied together with twine steeped in gum, which renders the blow heavier, and prevents it being softened in striking.

After the flagellation come the pincers, either cold or heated in a forge, of which the bellows are always going, so that they may be red-hot. They pinch a piece of the unfortunate martyr's flesh, and then drag and tear it off with a rapid movement or twist of the pincers, while the victim is tightly bound to the ground. This operation is renewed on the same individual five or six times. The agony inflicted by the pincers when cold is the greatest, but the wound is easier healed; whereas that made by the red hot pincers is very dangerous, the flesh around the burn generally festers, and the whole process seems to poison the blood; but it is less painful, because the burning deadens the nerves.

A fifth torture consists in forcing the confessor to kneel on a piece of wood full of pointed nails, of which the sharp points pierce through the joints and penetrate to the bone. The unhappy victim sighs pitifully during this protracted torture, while the mandarins laugh at his contortions, and add to his agonies by their fearful blasphemies against our Lord.

If the martyr has survived the infliction of all these horrors, they try a sixth method of torture, which consists of dragging him by his "cangue" to the cross, whilst they scourge him to compel him to trample it under his feet. If his lips still move in prayer, the executioners strike him on the mouth, and all the while outrage in the most disgusting manner the object of his veneration. Then the unhappy victims are again thrown into prison, heavily ironed, and separated the one from the other. The chains which they wear are composed of three pieces, of which one is fastened round the neck by a great ring, and the other two are fastened round the ancles by smaller rings, which are soldered to prevent the possibility of their being undone. They weigh five or six pounds. If it is too long you must hold it in your hand to be able to walk. If too short, you are constantly bent half double. After tortures like these, it is not surprising that the courage of the Christians should sometimes, though very seldom, fail, and these occasional apostasies add to the sorrow of the missionary, whose whole moral nature has been martyrized by the sight of such sufferings. Mgr. Retord declared that his sadness was immense, and that only the special grace of God could enable him to bear up against such misery. From Easter Day, 1858, nothing but misfortunes overwhelmed his diocese, and he gives a short summary of them in a letter to the Admiral Rigault de Genouilly, who had written to ask him for some account of the present state of things. After giving a graphic picture of the late persecution, he adds, "And now you ask what is become of us poor missionaries, Apostles in a field once so fertile, now so desolate and abandoned? I can hardly tell you. It is more than six months since I have received news of M. Néron, and I do not know where he is, or if he still lives. M. Galy started on an Annamite merchant-ship to implore the aid of the Spaniards of Manilla; but what is become of him I do not know. I fear he may have been assassinated at sea like P. Salgot. MM. Titaud, Theurel, and Vénard, finding themselves surrounded by the enemy in their little bamboo huts, escaped from them by night and took to the mountains. It is more than two months since I have had any tidings of them. Mgr. Jeantet, after wandering about in the hills for a long time, took refuge with some faithful peasants; and having to escape in the night, was nearly drowned in crossing a river. I have no news whatever of M. Saiget. As for MM. Charbonnier, Mathevon, and myself, who were at But-Son since the 13th of June, we have been living as we could; one day in a peasant's cabin, the next under the trees, or in the bushes, scrambling over impassable roads, exposed to a burning sun, or torrents of rain ; half dead with hunger, with scarcely any clothes to cover us, overwhelmed with fatigue and sorrow, not knowing from one hour to another what is to become of us, or where to lay our heads. Indeed, our tribulations have been unbelievable, and almost unbearable. For more than four months we have been unable to say Mass, having no vestments or altar, and no cabin where we can be quiet or in safety for half an hour. Hardly any of our native priests can say it either ; and what is worse, the sick die without receiving the last Sacraments. Every thing is dispersed, destroyed, or burnt; every one is in hiding ; hardly any one knows where I am, for I have no one to whom I can entrust a letter ; and the communications of others to me are lost, as the people are afraid of being compromised, and generally burn them. We are, in fact, reduced to the last extremity."

This sad letter was written in October, 1858. In December M. Vénard continued the recital of their sufferings in a long letter to his youngest brother, which we will transcribe literally.

"My dearest Eusebius,—I received in October last your letters and those of all my dear family of 1857 and 1858. You may fancy the joy they gave me. I wish I could, in reply, give you any consoling intelligence ; but, alas ! nothing but misery, tears, and agony have flooded this unhappy Annamite Mission for the last nine months. I wrote you word, in May, 1858, that the mandarins of Nam-Dinh had vented their satanic rage against the Christians by inventing unheard-of tortures, and that they had published a fresh edict against us more bloody than any that had preceded it. At that time the district inhabited by myself and M. Theurel was comparatively quiet; but the seizure of some letters, which we had written to the Christians of Nam-Dinh, by the mandarins, was the signal for the outburst of a more violent persecution than any we had before experienced. The bearer of our letters was put to the torture, and in his agonies owned every thing, betraying the sites of Mgr. Retord's new colleges of Vînh-Tri, Kê-Non, and Hoàng-Nghuyên. At the same time, the devil entered into the heart of one of our disciples, like another Judas, and he revealed to the mandarins not only the interior organization of the diocese, but all our hiding-places and means of escape from the persecutors. M. Theurel and I, although very anxious, flattered ourselves that, by stopping perfectly quiet, we might remain where we were; but the spies were too well informed. On the 10th of June, in the middle of the night, a Christian woke us hurriedly, to say that the troops were marching to surround our house and make us prisoners. It was therefore necessary to pack up our traps and fly. This was no easy matter. We were two Europeans, three Annamite fathers, ten or fifteen catechists, more than a hundred students, and had all the mission furniture besides, which was to be put in some place of safety. But our Annamites are so used to these sudden flights, that in a couple of hours every thing was hidden in different corners. On the morning of St. Barnabas' Day, the mandarin troops arrived to the number of 2000, while upwards of 1500 young pagans of the neighbourhood were told off to watch all the avenues to the college. In a few minutes they had surrounded not only the college itself, but three other villages near, the inhabitants of which were almost all Christians. They thought themselves, therefore, sure of their prey, and that they should catch the hare in her form. Happily, we had had warning in time, and had placed our poor students in distant villages; there were only two who had delayed their departure and were caught in the very act of escaping: they were instantly honoured with a 'cangue.' The soldiers had been promised a rich plunder, but found nothing but bare walls, and houses which looked as if they had been abandoned for ages. In their rage they spread themselves all over the surrounding country, and came upon a village which was precisely one where the greater part of our students had taken refuge, and where they would inevitably have been seized, if they had not received an early intimation of their danger. There were only about ten laggards, whom the soldiers came upon as they were flying across the fields, and whom they seized and tortured like the rest. Among these was an old deacon of upwards of seventy years of age. The mandarins, not being able to discover either catechists, priests, or students in the first four villages, carried off our poor old porter, a blind man, whom we employed to pick the rice, and a poor old woman and her daughter, who had the care of the church. The houses of the principal Christians were spared, owing to the intervention of the colonel and the sub-prefect, who were friendly towards us.

"Well, our mandarins returned in triumph with our dear prisoners, all wearing the 'cangue' round their necks, as criminals, and exposed to the derision of the pagans, as Jesus bore His Cross towards Calvary. This seizure was followed by several others, among whom were three Annamite priests, in all upwards of fifty persons. Our noble confessors had to endure frightful torments and scourgings; but all preferred death to apostasy. One of the mandarins tried to make a young catechist trample on the Cross. He replied, 'If you were told to trample under foot a coin bearing the image or superscription of the emperor, would you dare do it?' A great box on the ear was the answer. Another, taking the crucifix tenderly in his hand, and looking at it, said, 'Dear Lord! Thou hast never done me any thing but good, and they wish me to insult Thee! How could I have the heart?' Twenty strokes of the terrible 'rotin' were the reward of this outburst of love and piety. The mandarins ordered the students to chant their usual prayers. They intoned at once the litanies of the Saints, and when they came to the petition for the king and the mandarins, they repeated three times, with great fervour, 'Deliver them, O Lord, from all evil!' The mandarins understood the reproach, and commanded them to hold their tongues. Then they tried to compel the old woman and her daughter to apostatize; but they refused generously, and the old woman said, 'Who would be fool enough to walk on the head of his father and mother?' The judges, ashamed of being defeated by a simple old woman, sent her back to her village with her child.

"As to the rest, the three priests were beheaded; the two catechists and the poor old deacon died under the torture; and the rest were exiled to an unwholesome and wild mountainous district, where many have preceded, and will follow them. May our Lord support and strengthen them! They are fools for Christ's sake. Yet is theirs the only true wisdom. What they have sown here below in suffering and humiliation, they shall reap above in glory and in joy.

"Our churches, colleges, and houses have been burnt to the ground. Nor is this all. The Christians have been exposed to the most unjust and rapacious extortions. How can I describe to you what leeches these Annamite officials are, from the highest to the lowest? The first thing a mandarin does when he visits a province is to ask if the 'king's orders have been executed?' That is, in other words, 'Bring me some money.' When he leaves it is the same thing. Their underlings are worse. They quarter themselves upon the Christians, and if they do not at once give them all they ask, they denounce them to the authorities, who throw them into prison. The people may well give them the nickname of the 'mandarin horse-flies;' and what makes them more vexatious is the continual changes in these officials, and each one only looks upon his province as a place from which he must suck as much blood as possible in a short time. I have neither the time nor the heart to relate to you the turpitudes and villanies of these people, and that not to the Christians only, but to all who may be under their rule.

"The fate of our college of Hoàng-Nghuyên has been equally that of Kê-Non and Vinh-Tri, but the last has suffered most. I cannot tell you all the details, as our communications have been interrupted, and patrols placed on all the roads to prevent the Christians from meeting, or to compel them to trample the Cross under foot. But I know that out of 900 souls, thirty or forty of the principal people have been thrown into prison; that they have been tortured in the most horrible manner, yet that they have stood firm, and that a large number have been condemned to death; and it is not only Mgr. Retord's diocese that has suffered so terribly. The flood of persecution has swept over the whole country, from Cambogia to China. The Spanish Dominicans have been more cruelly treated even than ourselves. The order has come to seize all the Christians, and put them to death by what is called 'lang-tri;' that is, slow torture, cutting off first the ancles, then the knees, then the fingers, then the elbows, and so on till the victim is nothing but a mutilated trunk. Mgr. Melchior, the Dominican Vicar Apostolic of the eastern district of Tong King, was seized, and suffered this horrible death in August last. But you will ask me, 'How did you manage to escape the fury of a storm like this?' I can only reply, 'By God's grace, who has me in His holy keeping, and considers that my hour is not yet come. Our Christians keep guard round my cabin, and the only thing to do is to keep oneself in one little corner without speaking or making the least noise. Even a sneeze or a cough may betray you. We consider ourselves fortunate if, in these retreats, we can have a little hole for light, so as to be able to read our office and some comforting book. In this weary but voluntary imprisonment one has to learn patience, and give up one's life freely to Divine Providence. Then, if the mandarin seems to be inclined to search the house, one takes advantage of the darkness to escape to another hiding-place similar to the last. Sometimes we take advantage of a temporary lull, or a favourable moment, to take a little fresh air, and to stretch our cramped limbs. The chief misery of this state of things is, that one cannot administer the sacraments, and that a large number of our converts die without receiving any spiritual consolation. Another misfortune is that we almost always compromise the Christians who have given us hospitality, so that we often prefer trusting ourselves to the loyalty and good faith of some of the pagans, who are less suspected. M. Theurel and I stayed two days and two nights in one of these houses; but we did not see its owner, who kept himself hid, that he might not see a European face. We received notice to leave this asylum suddenly one night, and only a quarter of an hour afterwards the troops of the mandarins arrived to seize us. Mgr. Retord, seeing the way in which we were hunted from place to place, advised us to take refuge, as he and Mgr. Jeantet had done, in the mountain. We went; but the apostate before mentioned got an inkling of it, and surrounded the cavern where the Bishops had lately been concealed, having placed guards at all the mountain passes. But God watched over His faithful servants, and they escaped to the forests before the enemy had completed their preparations. The mandarins made perquisitions in all the caves, and carried off every thing they could find, which, in fact, was all that we possessed; but no one was taken prisoner.

"Mgr. Retord, M. Charbonnier, and M. Mathevon wandered barefoot through the woods, half dead with hunger, their feet wounded at every step by the pointed stones which the Annamites call *cats' ears*, and with no means of quenching their thirst but a villanous kind of water which no one can drink with impunity. Seeing no way of escape, they built themselves a little cabin in the centre of the forest, and remained there four months, during which time they were fed by the fidelity of the neighbouring Christians, and were preserved, in

spite of the danger they ran of being devoured by
bears and tigers. I sent one of my catechists
there in August, and he was met by a magnificent
royal tiger, who had that very day eaten two poor
girls who were pasturing their bullocks on the road-
side, and my poor catechist was only saved by a
miracle from a like fate. Dear brother, you will
want to know if Mgr. Retord be still in his forest
home? His body, yes; but his spirit has left this
vale of misery for a better world. A malignant
fever carried him off on the 22nd of October. Thus
ended this life of labour and of suffering, after
twenty-five years spent in the Missions, and fifteen
in the heavy labours of the Episcopate. He did
not live to see peace dawn on this unhappy country.
All his existence was spent amidst persecutions
and contradictions of all sorts; and was in truth a
realization of a dream he had as a child, in which
the Virgin appeared to him, and carried him to the
top of a high mountain, at the foot of a great Cross,
telling him that all his life would be a series of
crucifixions unto the end. All missionaries have
to follow the way of the Cross; but Mgr. Retord
did so more than any of us, and his death in the
midst of this terrible forest, exposed to the continual attacks of wild beasts, and without the com-
monest necessaries of life, was indeed the death
on the Cross,—as naked, as austere, as that of his
Lord and Master.

"When Mgr. Retord died he was alone with M.
Mathevon. M. Charbonnier having had a touch of
the fever, he had sent him down to be nursed in the
house of a pious Christian in the plains; and after
our holy chief pastor had expired, M. Mathevon
himself took shelter in a less unhealthy situation,
where he remains concealed. As for M. Theurel,
M. Titaud, and I, we too had to climb the moun-

tains, to walk with bleeding feet on the *cats' ears*, and to install ourselves as hermits in the forest. We remained there for a fortnight in perfect peace, and each day added some improvement to our Robinson Crusoe life. We collected rain-water to drink, and to cook our provisions; and we made a little straight avenue where we could walk and recite our office. Every morning the inhabitants of the village of Dông-Chiem brought us our provisions; and we had just begun to dig the ground and plant some vegetables, when one morning we received the unexpected surprise of a visit from six pagans, armed to the teeth, who came under pretence of tiger-hunting. We received them with great civility; and a few moments after, under pretence of going out into the adjoining forest to fetch some wood, we escaped rapidly down the mountain side to a boat which we kept on the river always ready for emergencies. These pretended hunters were in reality nothing but spies sent by the mandarins to find us out. From that moment we resolved to live in our boat amidst the reeds, now in one place, and now in another. A faithful and devoted young Christian brought us food every day, under pretence of fishing. This life of sea-birds went on for some weeks, when we found out we were again discovered and watched, which compelled us to separate, and seek shelter in different houses. I returned to my old district, and lived in the house of one of my catechists for three weeks, but amidst continual alarms; after which I took a lodging at But-Dong, in a convent, where I still remain. This village is half Christian, half pagan; and in case of alarm I have promised not to leave the place, but to take refuge in a cavern, which has been prepared for me. M. Saiget, who had been for three months in a dark place, escaped through a hole in the roof, and has been able to come and join me. Now we enjoy a certain tranquillity. The nuns have given us up their own room, which is large enough for us to walk six or seven steps, and two of our catechists are with us, so that we study Chinese together to fill up the time. But the spies of the mandarins surround us, and the poor nuns are in a continual terror. There are sixteen of them, and they take it by turns to watch day and night. On the other hand, it is an immense consolation to them to have the administration of the sacraments, confession, and communion, while we strive to console and strengthen them to the utmost of our power.

"We are in daily expectation of peace. A French squadron is arrived at Touranne on the 1st of September, and 3000 troops are camped on the shore. As soon as their arrival was known there was great rejoicing among both Christians and pagans; for the pagans hate the reigning dynasty, and attribute all the misfortunes of late years to the bad conduct of the king, who thinks of nothing but his pleasures, and neglects his people, whom he gives up to the oppression and rapacity of the mandarins. Many say, 'The cruelties against the Christians have brought down the vengeance of the gods on this dynasty. The Europeans come to deliver them, which is just and fair.' The appearance of a comet has strengthened the popular belief in the approaching dissolution of the Government. Such phenomena are always a sign of war to a superstitious people. A revolt has been organized, and only waits for the report of the success of the French troops to lift its standard from one end of the country to the other. Strangely enough, although the French squadron has been for three months and a half in Cochin-China, we have heard nothing."

A little later he writes, "The persecution goes on increasing in proportion as they imagine that the Christians have summoned the French to their assistance. When the comet waned, they put out an address to their divinity in these words: 'If the king and the mandarins have rendered themselves unworthy to govern this people, we ask thee, O wonderful Star, to remain visibly in the firmament: but if otherwise, then we adjure you to subdue your light and disappear.' Of course, in a few days the comet visibly decreased in brilliancy; and so these poor people imagined the king Tu Duc and his ministers had had a sign from Heaven! who would venture to doubt it?

"I have just heard that six more of our Christians have won the martyr's palm, of whom four were priests. One of our young students, of a rich and noble family, who had had the misfortune to apostatize under the torture, overwhelmed with remorse, gave himself up again into the hands of the cruel mandarin of Nam Dinh, who, in his fury, had him crushed to death under elephants' feet. Mgr. Jeantet says he was quite a little fellow, and in one of the youngest classes. He adds, 'Our older students were superhuman in faith and fortitude. One of them, covered with blood, said, smiling, to the torturers, "Your pincers and scourges are nothing to us; try something else!"'

"M. Legrand de la Lyraie, one of the missionaries in the eastern district, writes, as the interpreter of Admiral Rigault de Genouilly, who commands the French squadron in the Chinese waters, to implore us to take refuge on board his French steamer until the necessary measures be taken by the French army to deliver the Annamite Christians from oppression. The admiral is excessively alarmed at the dangers with which we are threatened, and wishes to put our lives, at any rate, out of the reach of the persecutors. Unfortunately, his proposal is impossible for us poor missionaries of the western district; we are too far from the sea, and all circulation in the country is too perilous to be attempted. I have answered M. Legrand's kind letter, and enclose this one in his, although there is always a fear that they will not reach their destination. I pray the Holy Angels to guard and conduct in peace the two devoted women who will be the bearers of my epistles! They are the universal letter-carriers, and manage it much better and with greater facility than men. Adieu."

This letter was dated December 21, 1858, and came to its destination in March, 1859, God having watched over the faithful messengers, so that they reached the French squadron at Touranne in safety. In July, 1859, similar letters were despatched by our faithful missionary; but they were intercepted, and never saw the soil of France. It was not till the month of March, 1860, that he again put pen to paper. But already the Reaper Death had been busy in his family; and his father had gone to announce to Heaven the coming of his son. His three children, grouped round his bed, implored his benediction. Mélanie, faithful to her promise, held up before his dying eyes the portrait of the absent one. "Dearest father, Théophane is also here; you must bless him with us." The poor father gave a deep sigh, and murmured faintly, "Ah, that dear child! where is he?" . . . . Then, gathering all his strength, and raising himself in his bed, he exclaimed, "Dear children, receive this the last blessing of your father, in the name of the Father, and of the Son, and of the Holy Ghost. Amen." And his uplifted hand fell heavily back on his bed. Then he looked upwards with such fixedness for some minutes that those around him thought he must have seen a beautiful vision; and so he slept sweetly in God, and his pure and honest soul passed without struggle to its rest. This beautiful death occurred at noon of Friday, the 26th of August, 1859, he being only sixty-four years old. His children had the following inscription engraved on his tomb:—

"Lord! He shared in Thy sacrifice; grant that he may share in Thy peace."

The sad news was at once conveyed to Tonquin, but the unhappy state of that country prevented the arrival of the letters; and Théophane never knew on earth of his father's death.

But to return to the Mission. After the death of Mgr. Retord, Mgr. Jeantet (who was upwards of seventy years of age) remained alone to administer that vast diocese. He therefore chose M. Theurel to act as his coadjutor; and this devoted missionary and bosom friend of Théophane's was accordingly consecrated Bishop of Acanthus, being only twenty-nine years old. If God had given peace for a short time to this persecuted Church, much might have been done by these two men, the one of such ripe wisdom and experience, the other with such fervent zeal and burning love of souls. But our Lord permitted the still further desolation of this land before the return of peace; and the following letter from F. Vénard will give us an account of the first and last persecution of which he was to be the witness and the victim. The letter is addressed to an old college friend, the Abbé Paziot, and is dated the 10th of May, 1860.

"My dear Friend,—It is a long time since I have written to you, and perhaps you may fancy I am dead, or that time has swept away our old

friendship. Now I hope both suppositions will
disappear when you see this monstrous bit of
paper (the only thing I can get), and on which I
shall try to paint for you (as I have nothing but a
brush) a description of our life here, in as good
language as a poor missionary can command who
has nearly forgotten his native tongue.

"I write to you from Tonquin, and from a little
dark hole, of which the only light is through the
crack of a partially-opened door, which just enables
me to trace these lines, and now and then to read
a few pages of a book. For one must be ever on
the watch. If the dog barks, or any stranger
passes, the door is instantly closed, and I prepare
to hide myself in a still lower hole, which has been
excavated in my temporary retreat. This is the
way I have lived for three months, sometimes
alone, sometimes in company with my dear old
friend, Mgr. Theurel, who has now been made
coadjutor to our Vicar Apostolic, under the title of
Bishop of Acanthus. The convent which sheltered
us before has been destroyed by the pagans, who
got wind of our being there. We had just time to
escape between two double walls about a foot wide.
From thence we saw through the chinks the band
of persecutors, with the mayor at their head,
garotting five or six of the oldest nuns, who had
been left behind when the younger ones took
flight. They beat these poor women with rods,
laying their hands on every thing they could get,
even to a few earthenware pots which hung on the
partition behind which we were concealed. And
we heard them vociferating, howling like very
demons, threatening to kill and burn every body
and every thing, unless they were given a large
sum of money. This agreeable visit lasted for four
hours; and there we were close to them, almost

touching them, not daring to make the smallest movement, and holding our breath till they were invited by the principal people of the village to go and eat and get drunk with them. Nevertheless, they did not go without leaving guards behind them, who surrounded the house; so that it was not till cock-crow in the morning that we could make our escape, and take refuge in a smoky dung-heap belonging to a pious old Christian widow, where we were joined by another missionary who had had equal difficulties in making good his retreat.

"What do you think of our position, dear old friend? Three missionaries, of whom one is a bishop, lying side by side, day and night, in a space of about a yard and a half square, our only light and means of breathing being three holes, the size of a little finger, made in the mud wall, which our poor old woman is obliged to conceal by some faggots thrown down outside. Under our feet is a brick cellar, constructed in the dead of night, with great skill, by one of our catechists; in this cellar there are three bamboo tubes, which are cleverly contrived to have their openings to the fresh air on the borders of a neighbouring lake. This same catechist has built two other hiding-places of the same sort in this village, with several double partition walls.

"We stayed with our poor old widow for three weeks, during which time I am afraid you would have been rather scandalized at our gaiety. When our three holes gave no more light, we had a little lamp, with a shade to prevent its tiny rays from penetrating outside through the chinks of our prison. One day we found ourselves surrounded, in fact completely blocked up, by sentinels posted at every corner of the house where we were, so that there was no possibility of passing from one house to the other. It was an apostate who had betrayed our hiding-place, and who knew we were in the village. Well, God defeated his plans. From morning till night, the pagans passed and repassed us, upset every thing in the houses, hunted in every corner. They broke in the outer walls, inside which we were concealed, and I thought our hour of martyrdom was come. But vain are the efforts of men when God opposes their designs! Perhaps you will say, In such a place, without air, light, or exercise, how can you live? Your question is perfectly reasonable; and, what is more, you might ask, Why don't we go mad? Always shut up in the thickness of two walls, with a roof one can touch with one's hand, our companions spiders, rats, and toads, always obliged to speak in a low voice, 'like the wind,' as the Annamites say, receiving every day the most terrible news of the torture and death of our fellow-missionaries, of the destruction of our missions, the exile of our students, and, worse still, occasionally, of their apostasy under the torture,—it requires, I own, a special grace, a grace fitted to our state, I suppose, not to be utterly discouraged and cast down. As to our health, we are like poor plants in cellars, stretching out our lanky, unhealthy branches towards the light and air. When I can put my mouth close to the door which guards our retreat, I own occasionally to a feeling of envy towards those who can enjoy God's fresh air and sunshine as much as they please. One of my brethren writes to me to-day to say, that for eighteen months he has not seen the sun; and he dates his letter 'from the land of moles.' As for me, I live on without being too bilious; the weak points about me are the nerves. I want something strengthening, like wine; but we have barely enough to say Mass, so one must not think of it. I have got now some pills, which an Annamite doctor has made up for me instead. Not many days ago, I managed to pass into a neighbouring house, and was very much astonished to find myself tottering like a drunken man. The fact was, I had lost the habit, and almost the power of walking, and the daylight made me giddy.

"I wrote to my family in 1858, to tell them of the French squadron at Touranne. In 1859 they destroyed the fortifications of Saigon, in Cochin-China, leaving a garrison in one of the forts of the river. Then came the summer, and news of the war with Austria, and a pestilential sickness, which began to decimate our troops. Nevertheless, hostilities were resumed against the Annamites in the autumn, and were continued till April, 1860, when, to the astonishment of every one, they retreated, and abandoned all the points they had previously occupied."

Then follows a long disquisition upon this retirement of the French troops, ending with, "Man proposes, and God disposes. An expedition undertaken by the iron will of the Emperor Napoleon III., and confided to such a man as Admiral Rigault de Genouilly, ought to have been crowned with success. But what are human probabilities to the Divine decrees? He has permitted that our deliverance should be delayed, and our Church still further purified by suffering. '*Attende Domine et miserere, quia peccavimus tibi.*' It is on account of our faults and shortcomings that these misfortunes have come upon us, and instead of blaming the cause, we should beat our breasts, and say, 'Have mercy on us, O Lord! according to Thy goodness.'

"The Annamite government seeing the French leave their shores, determined once for all to extirpate the Catholic Faith throughout the kingdom. Those mandarins who were in any way favourable to the Catholics were dismissed, and replaced by others whose hatred was well known. Crosses were placed at the entrance to all the villages, that the Christians might be forced by the guards to trample them under their feet. Then they chanted horrible blasphemous verses, declaring that *Zato*, which is the Annamite name of 'Jesus,' had a dog for his father, and men were found vile enough to carve crucifixes with a figure of a dog on one side and a woman on the other, so as to degrade to the utmost the God of the Christians." He then alludes to other horrors not fit for publication, and continues, "The government has established in each canton a new functionary, who is called 'The shepherd of the flock' (you may imagine he should rather be called the 'wolf'), and in each mayoralty an officer called 'the strong man of the village,' both of whom are employed in hunting down the unhappy '*Zato*,' or followers of Christ; who, being beyond the pale of law and justice, are exposed to every species of ignominy, suffering, and wrong, and that without a hope of redress. Then there is a curious law in this country, which makes a whole village suffer for the offence of one of its members. There, if a priest is found in a place, especially a European, the town is rased to the ground, half the inhabitants put to death, the rest scattered to the four winds, while the mayor or chief functionaries will be exiled and degraded if they have concealed the white man, or receive a large sum of money if they have betrayed him. Who could resist such a temptation?

"Again, from the destruction of our College, upwards of 1200 young men are on the wide world, without homes or occupation; not daring to return to their families, if they have any, and wandering from one Christian mission to another, till they almost inevitably fall into the hands of the persecutors. Scarcely one of these has yielded to the cruelty or blandishments of their tormentors, and the Church may indeed be proud of having engendered such noble confessors of the Faith. But you see, dear friend, how impossible it is for us, pastors of the flock, to console or break the bread of life to our poor suffering children. We are compelled to hide ourselves, and leave our lambs to the wolves. And then in this country the more insolent the nobles, the more cowardly the people, whom they treat as positive slaves. Their women, too, are treated as children without souls; and although they are models of chastity and of zeal for the Faith, they are so fearful that they almost lose their senses. It is only the nuns, who have had a longer and more careful Christian training, who can calmly brave the persecutors. When the French squadron appeared in 1859, the government persuaded themselves that it had been sent for by the missionaries, and that we were in league with the rebels to upset the reigning dynasty, and help on the revolution. They therefore seized the principal Christians in each village, and threw them into prison, which was a terrible blow to the poor and humble of the congregation, who had no longer any protectors whatever against their cruel oppressors. Out of seventy Annamite priests in this district, ten have already earned the martyr's palm; seven others are waiting in prison the moment when death will put an end to their torments. Upwards of 1000, both priests and laymen are exiled in the mountains. These are the valiant confessors whom God has chosen to glorify His name before the powers of the earth, and the thoughts of whom console us amidst all our tribulations.

"I began this letter in a little hiding-place in the midst of a fervent Christian population. In vain has the mandarin of the place (who has the hatred of a demon against Christ) employed every possible agent to destroy or weaken their faith. He has failed because the whole population is of one mind, and he cannot put them all to death. To revenge himself, he has sent bands of young pagans to announce his arrival, and to seize and gag the young girls, and commit every species of atrocity. Then when he does not come, they are only released on the payment of immense sums. So our wretched Christians are always on the *qui vive;* and to escape these horrors, men, women, and children escape to the rice-fields, and remain night and day concealed in mud and water. Sometimes the poor girls have been brought back to us half dead with the cold from this kind of exposure. One day the mandarin announced his visit, and his satellites were carrying on their work of pillage and brutality in every house. All of a sudden they discovered one of our hiding-places; which happily, however, was empty. They made a great row about this, and the next morning sent masons, with spades and hoes, to dig in every Christian house until they could find us. But Providence watched over us, and we made our escape; so that I am now in the midst of a pagan population, without knowing what is going to happen to me next. They appear kind and benevolent; but God alone can read to the bottom of their hearts. They have a high idea of hospitality, and would rarely wrong a stranger who has come so far to seek it. Perhaps God has chosen this way so that on them also the light of Gospel truth may shine. Dear old friend! as I write this, the thought of all our misfortunes has nearly overwhelmed me, and I can hardly restrain my tears. Before this terrible persecution our mission was so flourishing! so many souls were being garnered in! And now I feel like Jeremiah groaning over the ruins of Jerusalem. Will these ruins ever be rebuilt? It is like Ezekiel's vision of the dry bones. Can they ever be resuscitated? I have given you a summary of our misfortunes, but they are aggravated by a multitude of little circumstances which I should only weary you by enumerating. '*Magna est velut mare contritio tua! Quis medebitur tui?*'

"But as for myself, dearest friend, I have confidence in God that I shall accomplish my course, preserving intact the deposit of Faith, Hope, and Charity; and that finally, by the merits of our Lord, I shall share with His friends in the crown of the Just. I wrote to my father in June, 1859, but I fear the letter has never reached him. Send him this one, and let him feel it is as if written to himself; and ask him to redouble his prayers for his poor little child-missionary. Dear old father! He must be getting old now! I cannot help being anxious for tidings of them all, as for two years I have heard nothing.

"Dearest Mélanie,—I meant to have written you a separate letter, as also to my brothers; but this one must do for you all. I have had no news of you since December, 1858; but I do not doubt that you have written, and perhaps a few months' hence I may get your letters. À Dieu! and God

bless you, my much-loved ones. May you become greater saints day by day.—Your own devoted
"THEOPHANE.
"I commend myself specially to your prayers."

The contents of this letter, and especially its conclusion, point to the sad but glorious end which was at hand. The missionaries, hunted like wild beasts, could no longer find a place of shelter; and it is inconceivable how they could have so long borne such incredible calamities. In the meantime, M. Titaud, exhausted by the underground life he had been compelled to lead for two years, expired on the 29th January, 1860. M. Néron, betrayed by a traitor into the hands of the enemy, underwent the torture of the knout, and was then thrown into prison, where he remained for three months, of which twenty-one days were spent without any other nourishment than a few drops of water in the morning. At last he was beheaded, and thus fulfilled a curious prophecy which had been made him at Paris in 1848.

"M. Néron has left us," writes Mgr. Theurel, "and has passed from the battle-field to the rank of martyr; and M. Vénard is taking the same road, and will soon be with him in Heaven." But the acts of this heroic close to the life we have now been writing must form the subject of another chapter.

CHAPTER VIII.

The letter contained in the preceding chapter was written in the month of May, 1860. Of this time, Mgr. Theurel says,—

"M. Vénard was living in a pagan village, preaching and teaching with great success, although the people said that, to declare themselves Christians, they must wait till the persecution had a little ceased. The chief of the province having intimated that he considered him as his prisoner, M. Vénard went on to the Christian village of Kê-Bêo. He found superstitions of all kinds rampant in this place, and remained the longer, desiring, as he said, a hand-to-hand fight with the devil. God crowned his labours with wonderful success; and after a few months the whole aspect of the place was changed, and a fervent Christian population replaced the timid, superstitious flock whom he had found on his arrival. After this, he spent twenty days in the village of Kêm-Bâng, strengthening and consoling the terrified Christians, and incessantly employed in teaching and administering the Sacraments. From thence he went on to Bût-Sôn, one of our noted missions in this terrible thirty years' persecution. Here he found a devout native priest, and with him worked wonders among the people. Mgr. Jeantet joined him here; and a few days after, M. Vénard, leaving the venerable bishop in safety in this almost impregnable fortress, went back to Kê-Bêo. The good effects of his previous visit were still apparent; and M. Vénard thought he might remain in peace, and complete the good work. But he promised his catechist, Luông, that he would return very shortly to the safer refuge of Bût-Dông, as every one was extremely anxious about his safety. These were indeed critical days.

"On the 30th November, about nine o'clock in the morning, five or six junks, carrying about twenty men, appeared a few yards from the missionary's house. As it was an isolated one, and the inundations covered the whole country, these junks were able to guard every avenue. They were led by an old chief of a neighbouring hamlet, named Cai-Dô, the same who in 1854 had contrived the escape of M. Néron from the customhouse, but who now came on a totally different errand. Leaving his junks, he marched with five or six of his men to the mission house. M. Vénard, having understood the whole thing in an instant, had retired between the usual double walls. On arriving at the house, the chief cried out, 'Let the European priest come forth.' At these words, the catechist, Khang, who was busy hiding M. Vénard's property, came forward boldly, and said, 'It is I who inhabit this house, although I have only lately arrived. If you will leave me in peace, I shall be thankful; but if not, I shall be resigned.' The chief, giving a signal to his men to garrot the catechist, marched straight into the house, and giving a great kick to the thin double partition which concealed the missionary, seized M. Vénard, and dragged him brutally to the junks, with his servant. It was a very fine capture, accomplished with no risk whatever. By the time the faithful villagers of Kê-Bêo heard a rumour of the event, the junks were well out of sight with their prey, and a rescue was impossible. You will want to know, dear Eusebius, who was the Judas who betrayed our dearest brother and Christ's chosen minister. There are different versions, but the most probable is that which fixes the treachery on Sû-Dôi, a pagan, who was related to the widow with whom the missionary lodged.

"The chief, having carried off his prisoners in safety to his own home, made a great feast of rejoicing, after which he drove our dear missionary into a cage of bamboos, putting a 'cangue' on the neck of the catechist, and so took them to the prefecture. He stated that, when patrolling with his junks, he had come on these two men, who were without the jurisdiction of Kê-Bêo, and that he had hastened to bring them before the mandarin. This he said, because he hoped they would give him a large sum, and also because the chief of the village of Kê-Bêo was his son-in-law, who would either share the booty or lose his place. But his *ruse* did not answer; for every one knew that the missionary was at Kê-Bêo; and so that poor village was heavily mulcted, and had to pay upwards of 800 bars of silver, of which our poor community bore the half. From his cage, M. Vénard penned the following letter, which I insert in this one, and which runs as follows:—

"' *December* 3, 1860.

"'MY DEAREST PEOPLE,—God in His mercy has permitted me to fall into the hands of the wicked. On the Feast of St. Andrew I was put in a square cage and carried to the prefecture, from whence I trace these few lines for you, with some difficulty, with a paint-brush. To-morrow, December 4th, I am to appear before the judge. God knows what awaits me, but I do not fear. The grace of the Most High will be with me, and my Mother Mary will protect her poor little servant. I hope I shall be allowed writing materials; but I profit by this occasion, which a good pagan has given me, to send you my love from my prison. The household of the sub-prefect is full of kindness and attentions towards me, and so I suffer very little. They come and visit me continually, and allow me to speak freely; and I take advantage of the opportunity to instruct them in the Christian Faith. Many have owned to me their entire belief in our Creed, and say that the religion of Jesus Christ is the only one conformable to reason ; and that if it were not for fear of the king and his terrible edicts, they would gladly become Christians.

" Well, here I am in the arena of the Confessors for the Faith. Certainly God chooses the poor and weak things of this world to confound the mighty ! I have confidence that the news of my fight will be equally that of my victory, for I do not lean on my own strength, but on the strength of Him who has overcome the powers of death and hell. I think of you all, my dearest father, my beloved sister, and brothers ; and if I obtain the grace of martyrdom, oh, then still more shall I have you in remembrance! À Dieu, my best loved ones, to our meeting in Heaven ! In a moment I shall be adorned with the confessor's chains. Once more, adieu !' "

"The mandarin," continues Mgr. Theurel, "was very far from being pleased at the arrival of the prisoners. Like Pilate, he protested loudly against taking innocent blood, and declared that the sin and the odium would fall on the head of the takers, and that as for himself he only kept the prisoners because he did not dare let them go. He was most civil to M. Vénard, and changed his bamboo cage for a far more comfortable one in wood, both wider and higher, so that he could put himself in any position he pleased. He also had a very light chain made on purpose for him, weighing only two pounds and a half; and this valued chain is now in my possession ; our dear prisoner wore no other till his death. The prefect carried his condescension to the length of asking the missionary to dine in the audience-chamber like a free man. Then arrived a detachment of fifty or a hundred soldiers to escort the prisoners to the capital, and the prefect sent them with a long letter from himself, explaining the circumstances of their arrest by the Chief Dô, who formed part of the convoy."

Arrived at the capital, M. Vénard found means to write again to his family, and we give his letter in extenso:—

"*January* 2, 1861.

"My dearest Father, Sister, and Brothers, —I write to you at the beginning of this year, which will be my last on earth. I hope you got the little note which I wrote to you before, announcing my capture on the Feast of St. Andrew, when God permitted me to be betrayed by a traitor; but I owe him no grudge. From that village I sent you a few lines of farewell before I had the criminal's chain fastened on my feet and neck. I have kissed that chain, a true link which binds me to Jesus and Mary, and which I would not exchange for its weight in gold. The mandarin had the kindness to have a light one made on purpose for me, and treated me, during my stay in his prefecture, with every possible consideration. His brother came at least ten times to try and persuade me to trample the cross under foot rather than see me die so young! When I left the prefecture to go on to the capital, an immense crowd came to witness my departure; one of them, a young Christian, was not afraid to throw himself on his knees three times before my cage, imploring my blessing, and declaring me to be a messenger sent from Heaven, in spite of the guards and the mandarins. He was of course made prisoner.

"At the end of a couple of days I arrived at Kêcho, the ancient capital of the Tonquin kings. Can you fancy me sitting quietly in the midst of my wooden cage, borne by eight soldiers, in the midst of an innumerable crowd of people, who almost bar the passage of the troops. I heard some of them saying, 'What a pretty boy that European is!' 'He is gay and bright, as if he were going to a feast!' 'He doesn't look a bit afraid!' 'Certainly he can't have done any thing wrong!' 'He is come to our country to do us good, and yet they will put him to death!' &c., &c. We entered the citadel by the eastern gate, and they brought me at once before the tribunal of the judge in criminal cases. My catechist Khang, bearing his terrible 'cangue,' walked behind my cage. I prayed God's Holy Spirit to strengthen us both, and to speak by our mouths according to our Saviour's promise; and I invoked the Queen of Martyrs, and begged her to help her faithful child.

"'To begin with, the judge gave me a cup of tea! which I drank without ceremony in my cage. Then began the interrogatory as usual: 'From whence do you come?' 'I am from the Great West, from the country of France.'

"'What have you come to do in Annam?' 'I have come to preach the true religion to those who know it not.'

"'What is your age?' 'Thirty-one.' (The judge here said aside, with an accent of pity, 'Poor fellow! he is still very young!') Then he continued, 'Who sent you here?' 'Neither the king nor the mandarins of France; but it was I myself, who of my own accord came to preach the Gospel to the Heathen, and my superiors in religion assigned Annam to me as my district.'

"'Do you know the bishop called, in the Annamite language, *Liéow?*' (Mgr. Retord). 'Yes, I know him.'

"'Why did he give letters of recommendation to the rebel chiefs to enrol the Christians?'

"I venture to ask the mandarin in reply, 'From what source did he derive that information?'

"'The prefect of Nâm-Digne wrote us word of it.'

"'Well, then, I can bear witness that it is not true. The Bishop was too wise to commit so foolish an act, and if letters were produced to prove it I should know that they were false. I saw the circular which Bishop Liéow addressed to his priests, in which he positively forbid their joining the rebel chiefs, and declared that he would a thousand times sooner sacrifice his life than dip his crozier in blood.'

"'And the warriors of Europe, who took Touranne and Saïgon, who sent them? What was their object in making war on our country?'

"'Mandarin—I heard the rumours of war; but having no communication with these European troops, I cannot answer your question.'

"At this part of the interrogatory arrived the prefect, and hardly had he taken his seat when he cried out to me, in a loud and angry voice,—

"'Ah! you chief of the Christian religion, you have a clever countenance, you know very well that the Annamite laws forbid the entrance of the kingdom to Europeans; what was the use, then, of coming here to be killed? It is you who have excited the Europeans to make war upon us, is it not? speak the truth, or I will put you to the torture.'

"'Great mandarin, you ask me two things. To the first I reply that I am sent as an ambassador from Heaven to preach the true religion to those who scorn it not, no' matter in what kingdom, or in what place. We respect the authority of the the kings of the earth, but we respect more the authority of the King of Heaven. To your second question I answer that I never in any way invited or excited the Europeans to make war on the Annamite kingdom.'

"'In that case will you tell them to go? and you will then obtain your pardon.'

"'Great mandarin! I have no power and no authority in such matters, but if his Majesty sends me I will beg the European warriors to abstain from making war on the Annamites; and if I do not succeed, I will return here to suffer death.'

"'You do not fear death, then?'

"'Great mandarin! I do not fear death. I am come here to preach the true religion. I am guilty of no crime which deserves death. But if the Annamites kill me, I shall shed my blood with great joy for them.'

"'Have you any spite or ill-will against the man who betrayed and took you prisoner?'

"'None at all. The Christian religion forbids us to entertain anger, and teaches us to love those who hate us.'

"'Chief of the Christian religion! You must declare the names of all the places and people who have sheltered you up to this hour.'

"'Great mandarin! They call you the father and mother of this people. If I were to make such a declaration it would involve a large number of persons in untold misery. Judge for yourself whether it would become me to do this or not?'

"'Trample the cross under foot, then, and you shall not be put to death.'

"'How! I who have preached the Religion of the Cross all my life until this day, do you expect me to abjure it now? I do not esteem so highly the pleasures of this life as to be willing to buy the preservation of it by an apostasy.'

"'If death has such a charm in your eyes, why

did you hide yourself when there was a fear of your being taken?'

"'Great mandarin! Our religion forbids us to presume on our strength, and to deliver oneself over to the persecutors. But Heaven having permitted my arrest, I have confidence in Him that He will give me sufficient courage to suffer all torture, and be constant unto death.'

"This is a summary of the questions asked me, and of my answers. The mandarins then proceeded to question my catechist, and inflicted ten strokes of the knout, which he bore without flinching, God giving him strength all the while gloriously to confess the Faith.

"Since that day I have been placed in my cage at the door of the prefect's house, guarded by a company of Cochin-Chinese soldiers. A great many persons of rank came to visit and have conversations with me. They will have it that I am a doctor, an astronomer, a diviner, a prophet, from whom nothing is hid. A good many visitors have begged me to tell them their fortunes. Then they question me about Europe, about France, in fact, about the whole world. This gave me an opportunity for enlightening them a little upon points on which they are supremely ignorant, and on which they have sometimes the most comical ideas. I try above every thing to slip in a little serious word now and then, so as to teach them the way of salvation. But the Annamites are a frivolous race, and don't like serious subjects; still less will they treat on philosophy or religion. On the other hand, their heart is good; and they do their best to show me both interest and sympathy. My soldier guards have taken an affection for me; and though they have been blamed two or three times for letting me go out, they still open my cage

from time to time, and let me take a little walk. . . .
Sometimes their conversation is not very proper,
but I never pass over words of that sort; and sometimes, I do not hesitate to speak to them strongly.
I tell them that they lower themselves in the eyes
of every one by their impure thoughts and libertine
discourses; and that if they can talk in that way
without blushing, they deserve nothing but pity,
not to say contempt. My lessons make an impression. They are far more careful in their language, and some have gone to the length of begging my pardon for having made use of indelicate
expressions. Still I cannot say that every thing
is sweet and pleasant; although many are kind to
me, some insult and mock me, and say rude things
to me. May God forgive them!

"Now I am only waiting patiently for the day
when God will allow me to offer Him the sacrifice
of my blood. I do not regret this world; my soul
thirsts for the waters of eternal life. My exile is
over. I touch the soil of my real country; earth
vanishes, Heaven opens, I go to God. À Dieu,
dearest father, sister, brothers, do not mourn for
me, do not weep for me, live the years that are
yet left to you on earth in unity and love. Practice your religion; keep pure from all sin. One
day we shall meet each other again in Heaven, and
shall enjoy true happiness in the kingdom of God.
Adieu. I should like to write to each one separately, but I cannot: you know my heart. It is
three long weary years since I have heard from
you, and I know not who is taken or who is left.
Adieu. The prisoner of Jesus Christ salutes you.
In a very short time now the sacrifice will be consummated. God have you always in His holy
keeping. Amen."

His great friend Mgr. Theurel, the holy Bishop of Acanthus, took charge of this letter, and added, "The sentence of our dearest Théophane is pronounced. He is to be beheaded, but the execution will probably be delayed till the middle of February. In the meantime he wants for nothing. And though in chains, he is as gay in his cage as a little bird."

Mgr. Theurel continues,—

"As I was the nearest to Kêcho, being only one day's march from the capital, I was naturally able to write to him three or four times. Mgr. Jeantet and M. Saiget wrote likewise; and our dear prisoner was able to answer us pretty regularly. Our medium of communication was a native Christian, the head of the patrol, a man true as steel, named Huong-Moï, whose house had been my refuge for two months, and who had mingled with the troop of servants at the prefecture, and obtained his present post out of devotion to our sufferer. On the 28th December, Théophane wrote,—

"'The mandarins wrote four days ago to announce my capture to the king, but no answer has yet been received. They made me sign a written declaration of the circumstances of my arrest, countersigned by my catechist Khang. I have taken care that it shall compromise no one. I am pretty well treated, and some of the Cochin-Chinese soldiers are noble fellows. But I am kept at the door of the prefecture, so that I write with difficulty. The great mandarin allows threepence a day for my food, and I am pretty well in health. My heart is as tranquil as a lake which reflects the blue sky, and I have no fear. The mandarin of Nam-Xang (who spends his life in tormenting the Christians) came to see me the other day, and I told him that "Jesus was stronger than he; that it was in vain he struggled with our Lord; and that he would have to yield to His power in the end." The gaoler Tû (who seized four priests in 1859) asked after you. I told him publicly that "his was a vile trade; and that his diploma as mandarin of the ninth class, the price of treachery and blood, would fade as a wild-flower in spring," at which the mandarin, judge, and all the guards laughed and applauded. I think they like and respect me, and the great mandarin has twice invited me to dinner.'

"On the 3rd of January he wrote again: 'I have received your loving letter. A thousand thanks! I profit by the absence of the great mandarin to answer them. He used to allow threepence for my food, but now he has stopped it, so I should have gone supperless to bed to-day if the chief Maï, who is also in prison, had not sent me a bowl of rice. The new mandarin of justice came to see me yesterday, and put me through a fresh interrogation. When he said that the happiness of the next world was doubtful, while the joys of the present were certain and positive, I replied, "As for me, great mandarin, I find nothing on earth which gives real happiness; riches create envy and give cares; sensual pleasures engender endless maladies. My heart is too large, and nothing which you call happiness in this world satisfies it." On the whole, he was not uncivil. As he said he had given orders that I should be well treated, I replied that I had nothing to eat. He pretended not to understand me, so to-morrow the captain of the guard says he shall go and renew the demand. In spite of his fine speeches, this mandarin has doubled my guard, and sends some one constantly to see if my cage is closed. Among the gaolers is an excellent fellow named Tièn, who shows me the most affectionate respect. He alone, with one of the captains, is not afraid to make use of the expression "*Bám lay*," in speaking to me. (A term of reverence only used to mandarins, or persons of high consideration.) On New Year's Day the captain of the guard brought me a cup of first-class tea, and the gaoler Tièn passing at the time, I invited him to share it with me, which he did with a delicacy and a simplicity which only the heart could teach, and which hypocrisy could not counterfeit. But my letter runs on without a word as to one's feelings. I wrote a long letter to my family on very bad paper, but which I hope you received, and will kindly forward to them, filling up the details which may be wanting. Ah! I am now come to the hour so long desired by us all. It is no longer, as in the "Hymn for Departure," "*Perhaps* some day," but "*Very soon* all the blood in my veins

"Will be shed for Thee. My feet (oh, what joy!)
Are now loaded with chains."

"'In the long, weary hours in my cage I think of eternity. Time is, after all, so short when thus measured. You will repeat the words of St. Martin, "*Domine, si adhuc populo tuo sum necessarius, non recuso laborem;*" while I can exclaim with St. Paul, "*Jam delibor; et tempus resolutionis meæ instat;* (tibi) *vivere Christus est, mihi mori lucrum. O! quam gloriosum est regnum in quo cum Christo gaudent omnes sancti. . . . Audivi vocem . . . Beati mortui . . .*" (These are words that, in spite of the persecution, we never failed to sing on All Saints' and All Souls' Day, and which always touched us to tears.) I do not know if I shall ever be allowed to write to you again. Good-bye! I should have been very happy to have gone on working with you. I do so love this Tonquin mission! But now, in place of the sweat of my brow, I give them my blood. The sword hangs over my head, but I have no fears. Our good God has taken pity on my weakness, and filled me with Himself, so that I am happy, and even joyous. From time to time I astonish the mandarin's household by singing,—

> "O beloved mother,
>   Place me
>   Soon in our true home
>   Near thee!
> Noble Tonquin! land blessed by God!
>   Thou glorious country of the heroes of faith!
> I came to serve thee. I gladly die for thee.
> So be it, O Lord. Amen."

When my head falls under the axe of the executioner, receive it, O loving Jesus! O immaculate Mother! as the bunch of ripe grapes falls under the scissors, as the full-blown rose which has been gathered in your honour. *Ave Maria!* I will say this also from you. *Ave Maria!*' (I had begged him with earnestness to salute Mary for me on his arrival in Paradise.)

"'I should be very grateful if you could manage to send some remembrance of me to my family. My chalice was a family parting remembrance: if my brother Eusebius could have it, he would be in the seventh heaven of delight..... Oh, how glorious must be the kingdom in which the Saints rejoice with Jesus Christ our Lord! I heard a voice from Heaven saying, "Blessed are the dead that die in the Lord."'

"By this letter of the 3rd of January, from your brother," continues Mgr. Theurel, "you see the mandarins had ceased to feed the prisoner of Jesus Christ. This was what we expected; so we directly employed a Christian widow, named Nghiên, who happened to be a sister of the great mandarin's cook, to provide every thing that was necessary for him; and in that way we could have more frequent communications. On the 6th of January he wrote again:—

"'I have just received your good wishes for the new year. Thanks! Yes; for once I have indeed a lucky chance. "*Non volentis, neque currentis, sed miserentis est Dei.*" I ought to have sent you my affectionate wishes sooner, but you will forgive the delay. A happy new year to my dear, reverend Bishop! Peace and labour, and then an eternal repose in the bosom of the Saviour!... During the absence of the mandarin prefect, his wife, a young girl from Kêcho, recently married, came to pay me a visit; but when she saw me come out of my cage, she ran away like a child! I sent for her, and called her back as gently as I could; but when she did return, she was so frightened she could not open her mouth. Monseigneur, you must work at this—at the education of woman, to raise her from her present servile position, to establish schools for the young girls, to teach them the beauty and grandeur of Christian womanhood.... Let us say together once more, "*Tuus totus ego sum, et omnia mea tua sunt.*"'

"There was then in the prisons of Kêcho an Annamite priest, called Khoân, who is there still. I was in hopes that Théophane might have been allowed to see him; but their meeting seeming impossible, I sent the good Father Thinh, vicar of the parish of Kêcho, to comfort our dear prisoner. Huong Moï (that faithful head of the patrol whom I have before mentioned) undertook to introduce him into the mandarin's palace, and even to the cage of M. Vénard. The meeting took place on the 15th of January, in the presence of the guards and a whole crowd of people in the suite of the mandarins who filled the hall. Your brother, making believe not to recognize Father Thinh, asked the chief of the patrol, 'Who is that gentleman who came in with you just now?' 'It is the *thây-câ*,' replied Huong Moï. This expression signifies either a priest or the head of a family. Poor Father Thinh felt his heart sink into his shoes at this word. But Huong Moï, who laughed at danger, made jokes with the people round, so as to hide the confusion of the father and divert their attention elsewhere. M. Vénard, being formally introduced to him as to a stranger, was let out of his cage, and allowed to walk in the garden, where he instantly made his confession, none of the guards having followed him. When he came back to his cage, Huong Moï made a fresh and a successful effort to amuse the assistants, during which time Father Thinh approached the cage, as if for the purpose of examining it, and said a few words in a low voice to F. Vénard, giving him the absolution, and then walked away quietly. Your poor brother gave them all some tea, and then took leave of Father Thinh, who had brought the Blessed Sacrament with him, and left it with the devout widow, of whom I have spoken, who brought it to F. Vénard in the evening, concealed in some bread. He therefore could enjoy the presence of our dear Lord till midnight, after which he communicated. In a letter to Mgr. Jeantet, of the 20th January, he writes with emotion,—

"'Father Thinh will tell you of his visit, when I gave him some tea in the midst of all the crowd. He brought me, on the other hand, the Bread of the traveller,—"*Mi Jesu, Deus meus,*" in my cage! Think of that!' Then he goes on to say, 'I have not received a single stroke of the knout. I have received very little insult, and much sympathy; no one here wishes me to die. The people of the household of the great mandarin are kindness itself to me. I have suffered nothing, in comparison with my brethren. I have only to lay my head quietly on the block, under the axe of the executioner, and at once I shall find myself in presence of Our Lord, saying, "Here am I, O Lord! Thy little martyr!" I shall present my palm to Our Lady, and say, "Hail, Mary! my Mother and my Mistress, all hail!" And I shall take my place in the ranks of the thousands killed for the holy name of Jesus; and I shall intone the eternal Hosanna! Amen.'

"I enclose the last letters, written to you all, which are of the same date as mine, and which it is impossible, I think, for any one to read unmoved."

"I. M. I.
"FROM MY CAGE, KÊCHO,
"*January* 20, 1861.

"MY DEAREST, MUCH HONOURED, AND MUCH LOVED FATHER,—As my sentence is still delayed, I will send you one more word of farewell, which will probably be the last. These last days in my prison pass quietly: all those who surround me are civil and respectful, and a good many love me. From the great mandarin down to the humblest private soldier, every one regrets that the laws of the country condemn me to death. I have not been put to the torture like my brethren. A slight sabre-cut will separate my head from my body, like the spring flower, which the Master of the Garden gathers for His pleasure. We are all flowers planted on this earth, and which God gathers in His own good time; some a little sooner, some a little later. One is as the blushing rose, another the virginal lily, a third the humble violet. Let

us each strive to please Our Sovereign Lord and Master according to the gift and the sweetness which He has bestowed upon us. I wish you, my dearest father, a long, happy, and peaceable old age, and that you may bear the cross of life with Jesus unto the Calvary of a happy death. Father and son, may we meet in paradise. I, poor little moth, go first. Adieu! Your devoted and dutiful son,
"Théophane Vénard, Miss. Apost."

"I. M. I.
"From my Cage, in Tong King,
"*January* 20, 1861.

"My dearest Sister,—I wrote, some days ago, a general letter to the family, which I hope has reached you, and in which I gave all the details of my capture and interrogatory. Now, as my last hour is approaching, I want to send you, my darling sister and friend, a special word of love and farewell. For our hearts have been one from our childhood. You have never had a secret from me, nor I from you. When, as a school-boy, I used to have to leave home for college, it was my little Mélanie who prepared my box, and softened with her tender words the pain of parting. It was you who shared in the sorrows and joys of my college life; it was you who strengthened my vocation for the foreign missions. It was with you, dearest Mélanie, that I passed that solemn night of the 26th February, 1851, which was our last meeting upon earth, and which we spent in a conversation so full of intimate thoughts, and feelings of sympathy and holy hope, that it reminded me of the farewell of St. Benedict and St. Scholastica. And when I had crossed the seas, and came to water with sweat and blood this Annamite country, your letters were my strength, my joy, and my consolation. It is then only fair that, in this last hour, your brother should think of you, and send you a few last words of love and never-dying remembrance. . . . It is midnight. Round my wooden cage I see nothing but banners and long sabres. In one corner of the hall, where my cage is placed, a group of soldiers are playing at cards; another group at draughts. From time to time the sentries strike the hours of the night on their drums or 'tom-toms.' About two feet from my cage, a feeble oil-lamp throws a vacillating light on this sheet of Chinese paper, and enables me to trace these few lines. From day to day I expect my sentence. Perhaps to-morrow I shall be led to execution. Happy death, which conducts me to the portals of eternal life! According to all human probability, I shall be beheaded; a glorious shame, of which Heaven will be the price! At this news, darling sister, you will shed tears,—but they should be of joy! Think of your brother, with the aureole of the martyrs, and bearing in his hand the palm of victory! Only a few short hours, and my soul will quit this earth,—will finish her exile,—will have done with the fight. I shall mount upwards, and reach our own true home. There, in that abode of God's elect, I shall see what the eyes of man cannot imagine; hear harmonies which his ear cannot dream of now; enjoy a happiness which it has never entered into his heart even to conceive! But before arriving at all this, the grain of wheat must be ground,—the bunch of grapes must be trodden in the wine-press. May I become only pure bread and wine, fit for the Master's use! I hope it, through the mercies of my Saviour and Redeemer, through the protection of His Immaculate Mother. And so I venture, while still in

the arena, and in the midst of the fight, to intone
the hymn of triumph, as if I were sure of victory.
And you, my dearest sister, I leave you in the
field of virtues and good works. Reap a great
harvest of these for the eternal life which awaits
us both. Gather faith, hope, charity, patience,
gentleness, sweetness, perseverance, and a holy
death; and so we shall be together, now and for
evermore. Good-bye, my Mélanie! Good-bye, my
loved sister! Adieu! Your devoted brother,
"J. T. VÉNARD, Miss. Apost."

"I. M. I.
"*January* 20, 1861.

"MY DEAREST HENRY,—I must send you a few
lines also of brotherly love and farewell. You
were very young when we parted, and a stranger
to the world and its pleasures. Ah! the heart of
man is too large to be satisfied with the factitious
and passing joys here below, and I know you will
not seek for happiness where it is not to be found.
My dearest Henry, you are now twenty-nine, the
age of manhood. Be, then, a man. Do not waste
your life in the frivolities of the world. To resist
one's evil inclinations, to watch against the snare
of the Evil One, and to practise one's religion—this
it is which is to be really a man; not to do so, is to
be less than one. I write these words to you at a
solemn moment. In a few hours—at most, in a
few days—I shall be put to death for the faith in
Christ Jesus. Yes, my own dear brother, I die
with the conviction that you will always love God,
as you have loved Him in your childhood. He is
the God of your fathers, the God of those who
have given you life, the God of your brothers and
sister. He is the God whom the greatest intel-
lects humanity has ever known have served, wor-

shipped, and adored. He is the great and merciful God, the God who helps us to do right, and keeps us from evil—the God who alone will reward or punish us eternally.

"Read these words often; it is your best friend, your poor brother Théophane, who has written them. I leave to you the care of our dear father and sister. Be a good son, and a good brother; a good Christian, in life and in death! Good-bye, dearest brother. Come and meet me in Heaven. One who loves you,

"THÉOPHANE VÉNARD, Miss. Apost."

"I. M. I.
"*January* 20, 1861.

"MY MUCH-LOVED ONE,—If I did not write you a few lines for your very own self, you would be jealous, and, I own, with a very rational jealousy. You deserve it, too, for your many long and interesting letters to me. It is very long since I have heard from you now; and perhaps you are already a priest? and—who knows?—perhaps a missionary? However that may be, by the time you receive this your brother will be no longer in this bad world, *totus in maligno positus*. He will have left it for a better, where you must strive to rejoin him some day. Your brother's head will have fallen, and every drop of his blood will have been poured out for God. He will have died a martyr! That was the dream of my youth! When, as a little man of nine years old, I used to take my pet goat to browse on the slopes of Bel-Air, I used to devour the life and the death of the venerable Charles Cornay, and say to myself, 'And I, too, will go to Tonquin. And I, too, will be a martyr!' Oh, admirable thread of Divine Providence, which has guided me through the labyrinth of this life to this very mission of Tonquin and to martyrdom! Bless and praise our good and merciful God with me, dearest Eusebius, who has taken such care of his miserable little servant. *Attraxit me, miserans mei!*

"Dear Eusebius, I have loved, and still love, this Annamite people with an ardent affection. If God had given me long life, I would gladly have sacrificed every moment of it, body and soul, to the building up of this Tonquinese Church. The people are so good, so fervent, so loyal! If my health, feeble as a reed, did not enable me to do great things, at least I had my heart in the work. Man proposes, and God disposes: life and death are in His hand. As for us, if He gives us life, let us live for Him; if death, then let us die for Him.

"And for you, dearest little brother, still so young in years, you will remain long after me, fighting among the waves of this troublesome world. Guide your ship well. Let prudence take the helm, humility the rudder; God be your compass, Mary your anchor of hope. And then, in spite of the disgust and bitterness which, like a howling sea, will sometimes overwhelm you, never be cast down. Have confidence in God, and, like Noah's ark, swim always above the waters. . . . . My lamp gives no more light. Good-bye, my Eusebius, until the day when you come to rejoin me in Heaven. Your most affectionate brother,
"J. T. VÉNARD, Miss. Apost."

These letters were accompanied by a note from Mgr. Theurel, detailing the consummation of the sacrifice, which is as follows:—

"The 1st of February, M. Vénard wrote me another little note, which only reached me after his martyrdom. He says,—

"'The days of my pilgrimage lengthen out strangely. The prefect is astonished that my sentence should be so long delayed. All the despatches from the king pass before my cage. Each time I ask, 'if my sentence of death is come?' Each time the post-boy answers, 'No.' I hail each morning as the dawn of eternity; but evening comes, and I am still here. According to my reason and my heart, I hail the approach of death each day, but sometimes my presentiments seem to say that the answer will not be death; but I try to put this thought from me as a snare of the devil. Still the suspense is trying. Adieu, dear and loved Bishop of Acanthus! Will it be my last good-bye?—who knows? May the will of God be done, and not mine!'

"This farewell was really to be the last. In the night of the 2nd of February the desired sentence arrived at last; but M. Vénard knew it not. At two o'clock in the morning he breakfasted as usual, and then was allowed to go into the garden. The widow Nghiên, having followed him furtively, said, in a low voice, 'Father, you are to be executed to-day.' And because your brother doubted, as he had been told he was to be taken to the king, she added, 'It is quite certain. Already the elephants are ordered, and the soldiers ready; in a few moments you will be led to execution.' M. Vénard hastened to return to his cage to distribute his little things among his friends. At this moment an old lady name Xin arrived, bearing the Blessed Sacrament to the prisoner of Jesus Christ. This was the fourth time Father Thinh had been able to convey to him the Bread of Life. This pious lady, seeing that his moments were counted, pressed through the crowd of soldiers to the cage, and succeeded in putting into his hand the tiny box which contained the Sacred Host. But it was too great boldness. No sooner had the poor missionary received the treasure than the soldiers threw themselves upon him, dragged it from him by main force, and gave it to their captain. M. Vénard, forgetting every thing in his terror lest the Body of our Lord should be profaned, cried out to the widow Nghiên, '*They have carried off my Viaticum!*' The courageous widow ran to the captain who carried the box, and told him that this mysterious wafer was not, as he imagined, a poison to accelerate death, and anticipate the ends of justice, but a mysterious food for the passage from this life to another, and added, with a tone of conviction, 'If you venture to touch this Viaticum, you and all your family will die suddenly.'

"The captain, not knowing what to think of all this, timidly gave back the box to the widow, who, on account of the tumult, could not give it to M. Vénard. She therefore returned it to Mdlle. Xin, who sorrowfully, although safely, took it back to Father Thinh.

"Whilst these things were passing, the mandarin summoned the Confessor to hear his sentence, and send him to execution. M. Vénard had prepared himself a special dress for this the day of his nuptials, namely, a vest of white cotton with a long robe of black silk, which he wore on that day only. Having put it on, he appeared calmly before the mandarins; and, having heard his sentence, he took up his parable, and made a little speech. This was a formal declaration that he had only come to this country to teach the true religion, adding, that he was going to die for the same cause. He ended his speech by saying to his judges, '*One day we shall meet each other again, at the tribunal of God.*' The mandarin of justice rose hastily, and exclaimed, 'I will have no insolence!' and the convoy was ordered to start at once. It was composed of two elephants and two hundred soldiers, commanded by a lieutenant-colonel. M. Vénard commenced singing Latin psalms and hymns as the procession passed through the town. The place of execution was about half an hour from the mandarin's house, and when they had arrived, the soldiers formed a great circle round him to keep back the crowd, which was enormous; but the courageous widow Nghiên broke through their ranks, and at last obtained permission to remain with him to the end.

"M. Vénard, with a calm and even joyous countenance, looked all over the crowd, hoping to see Father Thinh, and to receive a last absolution. But this poor father, not knowing of the order for the execution having arrived, could not get there in time. Your brother then, having given his sandals to the faithful widow, sat quietly on his mat. They took off his chain, having with a hammer undone the nails which fastened the ring round his neck and ancles, and then the soldiers pushed even the poor widow outside the circle.

"The executioner was a horrible hunchback, called Tûe, once an old soldier, and now an actor, who had already decapitated four of our priests on the 25th of March, 1860. He had begged to be allowed to perform this horrible office that he might have the martyr's clothes. He began by asking him, as to an ordinary criminal, 'What he would give him to be executed promptly and well?' But the answer he received was, '*The longer it lasts the better it will be!*' Seeing that M. Vénard's clothes were new and clean, his whole anxiety was to get them without any stains of blood. He therefore begged his victim to strip; and, as this first invitation remained unheeded, with barbarous ingenuity, he added,

'You are to be *lang-tri*,' that is, have all your members cut off at the joints, and the trunk sawn in four. Then our dear missionary, either because he believed the lie, or to imitate more nearly the humiliation of our dear Lord and Saviour, who before His crucifixion bore the same treatment, and perhaps also to get rid of the importunities of this vile hunchback, took off all his clothes save his trousers. Then his elbows were tightly tied behind his back, so as to force him to hold up his head for the fatal stroke, and he was fastened to a stake which was badly fixed to the ground. In this position, at a given signal, M. Vénard received the first fatal stroke—but it was only a trial one on the part of the barbarous executioner, and only cut through the first skin. The next stroke, more vigorously applied, cut off half the head, and knocked down the stake and the missionary together. Then the executioner, finding that his sword was blunt, took another, and cut and hacked at his neck, amidst the indignant murmurs of the crowd; after which, having seized the head by the ear, he held it up to the lieutenant-colonel who presided at the torture. This officer, having desired the municipal authorities to keep watch for three days, during which time the head was to be exposed, instantly sounded the retreat, and marched his troops back to their quarters. During this time the poor widow Nghiên and a great number of the spectators bewailed and lamented themselves as if at the death of their first-born. No sooner had the troops left the ground than the crowd and the women precipitated themselves on the spot to soak their handkerchiefs and papers in the martyr's blood; and such ardour did they show that not a blade of grass was left in the place. The execution had not taken place on the ordinary spot. The great mandarin had desired that the missionary should be beheaded on the edge of the river, so that the head might be thrown into it with greater ease after the exposition. For this reason many of the curious, and likewise of the faithful, had gone a wrong road, and amongst the rest a good pagan who had undertaken the burial of the body; so though the execution had taken place at eight in the morning, at midday it still remained extended on the sand, covered with a mat. Then, a bier having been brought down the stream, every thing was prepared for the interment. Besides the family of this faithful pagan, Huông-Da, the widow Nghiên, had not left the remains for an instant. It was also watched by a Christian mayor of a neighbouring village, named Ly-Vûng, and a devout Catholic boatman from the southern district of Tonquin. This last had the delicacy to wrap the martyr's body in his own coat, which he took off for that purpose. The whole was afterwards wrapt in a cotton sheet, tightly bound round with three linen bands, so as to be able to lift it up later, and then buried, for the same reason, in a coffin only a foot deep. The head remained, which had been placed in a little wooden box at the top of a pole. The mayor Ly-Vûng had made one exactly similar, in order to try and substitute the one for the other, and get possession of the precious relics. But it was found impossible to cheat the vigilance of the guards. Our only hope then was to resort to some other expedient. The gaoler, charged with the care of the head, was promised a silver bar if he would let us throw it into the river in our own way. This man, nothing loth, came at the dead of night, on the fourth day, to facilitate the matter. But God permitted that our plans should be contravened by a little mandarin of Balliage, a young wolf of twenty-three, whose only idea of government was to devour his people, which his blood royal enabled him to do with impunity. This man sent one of his household to superintend the projection of the head into the water. Our old friend, Huong-Moï, had fastened a fish-hook in the ear, with two hundred yards of line and a floater, and persuaded the mayor to throw it all together into the river, thinking that the float would enable us to discover it easily on the morrow. But the frightened mayor threw the head in without detaching the line from the boat, and after pulling a few strokes (the head naturally following), on the alarm that the mandarin was coming, shook the line violently to get rid of it, and the hook got loose, so that the head sunk to the bottom of the stream. All our endeavours to recover it the next day were in vain. But God managed it for us in another way. On the 15th of February some Pagan friends of Ly-Vûng, rowing down the stream, perceived something floating on the water about four leagues from the place of execution. They took it up, and found it to be our dear martyr's head. The good mayor, Ly-Vûng, hastened to take it to his house, and send for Father Thinh, who instantly recognized it, and put it carefully in a white silk bag in a vase, which they fastened down with tar. The good father having sent me word of what had occurred, I desired him to bring it to me, and the precious relic arrived on the 24th of February. I opened the vase in presence of five witnesses : it was incorrupt. I took the little white bag in which Ly-Vûng had enveloped it, and in which it had laid for nine days ; from the right ear I took out the fish-hook which Huong-Moï had fastened in it, and which remained in it with about an inch of the line. It had made a wide opening in the ear, as by a violent wrench. The state of the flesh round the ear showed how it had been hacked by the inhuman executioner. I cut off some of the hair with my scissors, keeping five or six locks for his family. I tearfully turned and returned this much-loved head in my hands, and finally replaced it in its urn, and interred it in a neighbouring house according to the earnest entreaty of the inhabitants; finding it impossible at this moment to do with safety what I had wished, namely, to reunite the head to the other members. For this we must wait for a time of peace."

The last sacrifice was thus consummated, the victim immolated, and the holy martyr had gone to receive in Heaven the reward he had so ardently desired. There he would be met by his father and his mother, the one having preceded him eighteen years, and the other eighteen months. Mgr. Jeantet, fancying his father was still alive, wrote to comfort him by speaking of this joyous meeting with his mother, and declared that Théophane, by his great merits, had well deserved the martyr's palm; adding that the Blessed Virgin, to whom he had ever been so tenderly devoted, had thus glorified him in the eyes of the whole world. But to conclude Mgr. Theurel's account,—

"My dear friends, am I to tell you that we are rejoiced or afflicted at your dear brother's glorious end? In one sense we all rejoice at his triumph, blessing and praising God for His choice; but for my own part, I cannot help feeling deeply the separation which has taken place. I am still quite young: the same age as our dear Théophane; our warm friendship, and an entire conformity of views on all points, made him a powerful auxiliary in all my labours, and a sharer in all the cares and anxieties of the future. Your brother was at least one-half of my strength and of my courage. He had the greatest prudence and wisdom, united with a burning love and zeal; it seemed as if he and I together could do great things in this Tonquin vineyard; but alone, how shall I get on? His departure has cast me down terribly, and has upset all my hopes and plans. I have cried for him bitterly, and shall cry still more, whatever people may say! I have said that he had an immense zeal for souls; also, although his health was more delicate than that of any other missionary in the diocese, he did more work than any body else, passing half the night, and sometimes the whole day besides, in the confessional. His confidence in God was boundless, and made him bold almost to a fault in his undertakings. Whilst he was working so admirably at Kê-Bêo in the month of June, I wrote him word that he must take greater precautions, for that the heavens were big with clouds. He answered me with that frank and holy boldness which was one of his characteristics, that not a hair of his head would fall without the will of God. And, in truth, our Lord had determined the hour of his martyrdom, and his happy fate was foretold him in 1851. He was likewise a wonderful linguist, and had completely mastered the difficult Annamite dialect. He translated the '*Concordantia Evangelica*' of M. Migne into good Annamite, as well as the Acts of the Apostles. He had just completed the translation of the Epistles and of the Apocalypse; and was in the midst of an abridged Commentary from that of Picquigny, when he was seized. These two last translations, of which no one had a copy, have, to my great despair, been burnt, not by the chief who took him prisoner, but by the Christians of Kébés, whose fears had really troubled their reason. Another of our Christian missions has been more faithful to the memory of our dear brother. I mean that of Bût-Dông, where he lived for eighteen months with M. Saiget. This whole parish has been for upwards of a year in open war with the mandarin, Nam-Xang, whom your brother apostrophized so vehemently from his cage. This functionary came himself to Bût-Dông to force the people to trample the cross under foot; but the whole population having unanimously refused to apostatize, he was forced to yield to the resistance of 1800 men; and although since then he has issued edict after edict, he has done nothing but lose both his time and his trouble. . . . . Mgr. Jeantet wrote to our dearest Théophane, hoping that when the time came for the re-establishment of the seminary, he would undertake the office of Professor of Theology. 'I hoped so much,' writes his Grace, 'from his wonderful piety, zeal, and science. But the Sovereign arbiter of all things has decided otherwise—"*Fiat voluntas tua.*"' The holy widow Nghien," continues Mgr. Theurel, "brought back the clothes and chain of our dear brother, and transmitted the whole faithfully to us. A little later we hope to send to Paris the chain, the little bag, and the fishhook of which I have spoken, together with the hair, one or two autograph letters of the martyr, and the linen soaked with his blood. The ring which went round the neck is wanting to the chain, having been appropriated by the brother of the mandarin, as also one of the feet rings. I will send you, my dear Eusebius, as well as to M. Henry and Mdlle. Mélanie, your portion of his hair, and of the linen soaked with his blood. I do not send these things to-day, as my parcel is already too heavy; it must be for the next time. A little later I hope also to send you each some little remembrance chosen from among his things. Mgr. Jeantet and I, and I doubt not all our brethren, will consent that his precious martyr's chalice should pass into your hands.

"The catechist, Khang, who was taken with your brother, was exiled into the province of Hông-Hôa, which belongs to the Western Vicariate. But before starting, he was allowed to go and venerate the head of his Spiritual Father, which was still exposed. This was on the 4th of February. The chief of the Canton Dô, besides the recompense he received of thirty bars given by the king, received four bars from the mandarin prefect, and has been created a mandarin of the ninth class.

"After the martyrdom of your dear brother, I learnt the news of your father's death, so that I do not address this letter to him, but to you all. . . . *Beati qui lavant stolas suas in sanguine Agni!*"

(*Note of the Family.*—Mgr. Theurel wrote as follows on the 25th of March, 1865, on the subject of the relics, to M. l'Abbé Eusebius Vénard, Vicar of the Cathedral at Poictiers:—" The whole of your dear brother's body, except the head, is arrived at Hong Kong on the 1st of March, and started for France by the ship 'St. Vincent de Paul.' It will arrive the end of August or the beginning of September, by Nantes. With the body I have sent the chalice and other precious little remembrances."

In the same cover, Mgr. Theurel, foreseeing our impatience, sent us each a portion of his relics, contained in three little packets, sealed with the Episcopal Seal, and the following inscriptions, written in his Grace's own hand:—*Hair of M. T. Vénard. Linen imbibed with his blood. Small bones, cartilage, nails, &c.*)

CHAPTER IX.

The official news of the triumph of the illustrious martyr did not arrive in France till the end of December, 1861, nearly eleven months after the event; and Mgr. the Bishop of Poictiers at once resolved to hold a feast in honour of one whom his hand had introduced to the sanctuary, and who had become the glory of his diocese by his heroic confession of the Faith and the shedding of his blood for Jesus Christ.

The feast was fixed for Sunday, the 2nd of February, being the day of the Purification of the Blessed Virgin, and the anniversary of the martyrdom. The bishop came himself to preside at the ceremony in the church of St. Loup, the native parish of our hero. He was accompanied not only by the members of his own chapter, but by about a hundred priests, old friends or companions of Théophane, including l'Abbé Dallet, who had been compelled from bad health to return to France for a few months, and the Superior of the Seminary of Foreign Missions at Paris.

After the benediction of the candles, the bishop gave the signal for the procession; and it seemed as if each priest bearing his taper had said, "See how your Théophane has shone with a pure and vivid light, and thus justified his name." After the Mass, the bishop preached, and that with such fervour and emotion that the whole audience melted with tears. Yet was there nothing sad about the festival. As M. l'Abbé Pauvert said, "In each martyr, grace assumes a different character. In Théophane it was an indomitable serenity, a joyous calmness which nothing could disturb. One may say of him as the English do of one of their poets, 'That he was born with a rose-bud on his lips, and a bird to sing in his ear;" so graceful was his imagery, so melodious his words. His natural sweetness spread a charm over every thing and every one with whom he came in contact. Even at the last moment of his life he poured it out on those who pressed round his cage, on the instrument of his torture, on the very earth which was to drink his blood. We feel as if the fatal blow which severed that dear and honoured head were only as the pressure which separates from its stalk the fair flower which is to adorn the altar." This joyous calmness in the martyr's character, so well known to his parents and fellow-citizens, had coloured the festival held in his honour. Nothing spoke of death, but every thing breathed hope and life.

His father's house was decked with flowers, as on a marriage feast; and at the breakfast given by his brothers, the room was decked with festoons and garlands, and the cypher of the martyr, entwined with palm branches and crowns.

Mdlle. Mélanie Vénard assisted at the feast. She had now followed her heart's desire (so often talked over with her martyred brother), and had taken the veil in the Convent of the Holy Family, under the name of "Sister Théophane."

Towards the end of dinner, the Abbé Chauvin, Vicar of St. Jacques de Châtelleraut, read a hymn in honour of the martyr, the graceful and tender poetry of which provoked murmurs of approbation from the bishop and all the assembled company. Between the services, a large number of Théophane's old friends made a pilgrimage to the grassy hill-sides of Bel-Air, where the first inspiration of going to the Foreign Missions had come into his childish heart, and where his friends are now about to build a little commemorative chapel in his honour.

The wax taper carried by the bishop on that occasion, and ornamented with palms, was laid up by his desire as a memorial in the parish church, and by its side hangs a square frame containing an autograph letter of the martyr, written with a paint brush in his cage.

And now that my readers have followed Théophane from his birth to his death, is their interest in him entirely at an end? If our minds have been for a short time turned from the frivolous thoughts of every day to the contemplation of a life so pure, so holy, so single-minded in the dedication of all its gifts and powers to God, will it not have some influence, some effect on our future conduct?

We feel confident that our Lord will not allow so eminent an example to pass unheeded, and that already Théophane's words have kindled in other souls a like burning love and zeal for the conversion of the heathen. Scarcely had he reached China, when his letters fired the ambition of many of his old friends and companions, and determined them to share in his Apostolic labours for the Foreign Missions. We trust that on those who read this little book a like impression may be made: that if all cannot actually take a part in the missionary's life, they may at least help others to do so by propagating the works of the Foreign Missions to the utmost of their power in the circle of their own homes. Already at the Congress of Malines a noted Catholic orator, M. Augustin Cochin, after having pronounced an eloquent discourse on the progress of science and arts in the religious point of view, quoted a letter of Théophane's to enforce his arguments, and to induce the eminent men who listened to him to join in a series of resolutions, of which the first was, "To labour incessantly for the *Propagation of the Faith among the Heathen.*" He went on to say, "I cannot understand that any true Catholic should refuse to labour energetically for the maintenance of those model men amongst us, who go forth to regions where the Gospel is unknown, and seal the truth with their blood. Their words breathe a faith and an ardent charity of which their lives and their deaths are the proof. . . .

"I was struck the other day by an unexpected coincidence between the letters of two men to their sisters; the one in the presence of death, the other to one already dead. The latter was from a man, but too well known now, and who, searching in his heart for that which was purest and best, could only speak of 'refined doubts,' 'delicate questions,' 'of tears mingled by the women of old with the waves of Biblos,' 'of the mysteries of Adonis,' .... and he writes this to her whom he calls his 'good genius!' The former written at midnight from his cage on the eve of his martyrdom, on the 20th of January, only two years ago (at the very moment, gentlemen, when some of us were probably at a ball)." . . . (He then read out the letter to Mélanie which we know, and added) "Gentlemen, between these two letters of Rénan and Théophane Vénard, between the two doctrines they inspire, between the two states of mind which they reveal, my choice is made; and therefore it is that I so earnestly recommend to you the work of the propagation of the Faith!"

The whole Congress was moved by these eloquent words; and the letter, which M. Cochin termed "One of the most beautiful pages of the History of the Martyrs of the Nineteenth Century," produced in the hearts of his 3000 auditors an emotion which bore immediate fruit, for the next day the orator received, among many other offerings, in an envelope, but without any signature or sign of the donor, a bank note for 1000 francs for the Foreign Missionary College.

Let us hope that this generous heart may find its imitators; and that this humble biography, however feebly executed, may move other Christian souls to come forward and help in this great work. The treaty of peace is now concluded between France and Cochin-China. The ferocious Tû-Duc has repealed his persecuting edicts, and published a decree announcing entire religious liberty in the kingdom of Anuam. The wished-for day has, therefore, dawned when a fresh band of Apostolic workers may start for this land, to replace those who have fallen under the axe of the executioner, and reap an abundant harvest in this field of our Heavenly Father's, where the seed has been so long sown in tears and blood. Thus will Théophane Vénard, whose whole life was so devoted to this Tonquin Church, see the "travail of his soul, and be satisfied;" and in the glorious fruition of his labours reap the reward of the elect in the Kingdom of God.

Appendix.

APPENDIX.

CHANT POUR LE DÉPART DES MISSIONNAIRES

(DU SÉMINAIRE DES MISSIONS ÉTRANGÈRES).

"Quam speciosi pedes evangelizantium pacem, evangelizantium bona."

Paroles de M. D***.   *Musique de M. Ch. Gounod.*

Qu'un souffle heureux vienne enfler votre voile,
Amis, volez sur les ailes des vents,
Ne craignez pas, Marie est votre étoile,
Elle saura veiller sur ses enfants.
Respecte, ô mer ! leur mission sublime,
Garde-les bien, sois pour eux sans écueil,
Et sous ces pieds qu'un si beau zèle anime,
　De tes flots abaisse l'orgueil.

　　Partez, amis, &c.

Hâtez vos pas vers ces peuples immenses ;
Ils sont plongés dans une froide nuit.
Sans vérité, sans Dieu, sans espérances ;
Infortunés ! l'enfer les engloutit.
Soldats du Christ ! soumettez-lui la terre,
Que tous les lieux entendent votre voix,
Portez partout la divine lumière,
    Partout l'étendard de la croix.

    Partez, amis, &c.

Empressez-vous dans la sainte carrière,
Donnez à Dieu vos peines, vos sueurs,
Vous souffrirez, et votre vie entière
S'écoulera dans de rudes labeurs.
Peut-être aussi, tout le sang de vos veines
Sera versé ; vos pieds, ces pieds si beaux,
Peut-être un jour seront chargés de chaînes,
    Et vos corps livrés aux bourreaux.

    Partez, amis, &c.

Partez, partez, car nos frères succombent,
Le temps, la mort, ont décimé leurs rangs ;
Ne faut-il pas remplacer ceux qui tombent
Sous le couteau de féroces tyrans ?
Heureux amis ! partagez leur victoire,
Suivez toujours les traces de leurs pas ;
Dieu vous appelle, et du sein de la gloire
    Nos martyrs vous tendent les bras.

    Partez, amis, &c.

Soyez remplis du zèle apostolique ;
La pauvreté, les travaux, les combats,
La mort : voilà l'avenir magnifique
Que notre Dieu réserve à ses soldats.
Mais parmi nous il n'est point de cœur lâche,
À son appel tous nous obéirons,
Nous braverons et la cangue et la hache,
    Oui, s'il faut mourir, nous mourrons.

    Partez, amis, &c.

Bientôt, bientôt, nous courrons sur vos traces,
Cherchant partout une âme à convertir ;
Nous franchirons ces immenses espaces,
Et nous irons tous prêcher et mourir.
Oh ! le beau jour, quand le Roi des Apôtres
Viendra combler le désir de nos cœurs,
Récompenser vos travaux et les nôtres,
   Et nous proclamer tous vainqueurs !

  Partez, amis, &c.

En nous quittant vous demeurez nos frères,
Pensez à nous, devant Dieu, chaque jour ;
Restons unis par de saintes prières,
Restons unis dans son divin amour.
O Dieu Jésus notre roi, notre maître,
Protégez-nous, veillez sur notre sort,
À vous nos cœurs, notre sang, tout notre être,
   A vous, à la vie, à la mort.

  Partez, amis, adieu pour cette vie,
  Portez au loin le nom de notre Dieu,
Nous nous retrouverons un jour dans la patrie,
   Adieu, frères, adieu.

THE MISSIONARY HYMN.

(FROM THE FRENCH.)

Translated by the VERY REVEREND CANON OAKELEY.

I.

HERALDS of Peace! away, away,
  Speed blithely o'er the main;
No voice shall now your progress stay;
  No bonds your zeal enchain.
This is the day, the wished-for day;
Heralds of Peace! away, away.

II.

How beauteous shine the feet of those
  Who spread the Word of Life,
And treasures of the Cross disclose
  In lands where sin is rife!
With duteous love, and reverence meet,
We kiss, dear friends, those sacred feet.

III.

We part to meet again no more
  This nether side of Heaven;
But look for greeting on that shore
  Where friendships ne'er are riven.
With words of love and hearts of flame
Bear to the lost their Saviour's name.

IV.

May no rough breeze your courses mar,
    No mists your steps benight,
Beam o'er your path the ocean's Star,
    And Christ be all your Light.
With words of love and hearts of flame
Bear to the lost their Saviour's name.

V.

Those darksome realms your advent wait,
    Where sin and Satan dwell;
Where vengeance rages at the gate;
    Where yawns the pit of Hell.
Bereft of hope and God they lie,
Beside a deep eternity.

VI.

Soldiers of Christ, subdue the world;
    He claims it for His own.
Be every where His flag unfurl'd,
    So He may reign alone.
With words of love and hearts of flame
Bear to the lost their Saviour's name.

VII.

Speed, brothers, speed, though toil and pain
    Your onward course surround:
Where life is Christ, there death is gain,
    Life lost is glory found.
Earth's loss is gain, earth's gain but loss;
Who seeks the crown, must bear the cross.

VIII.

The blood that mantles in your veins
    For Christ shall haply flow;
And tortures bind with cramping chains
    The feet at which we bow;
And bones be crush'd, and flesh be torn,
Mid tyrants' rage and people's scorn.

IX.

Go, claim the place and fill the void
  By bonds and death created;
Repair the loss of friends destroy'd,
  Of armies decimated;
Christ calls you, and our martyrs love
To greet you in the courts above.

X.

Be we with Christian zeal replete,
  And Apostolic fire,
Then labours, sufferings, death, are sweet,
  Yea, objects of desire;
For earthly crowns earth's soldiers strive,
But we, that dying we may live.

XI.

The biting axe, the halter cord,
  We scorn them and defy;
If death or safety be the word,
  Then we will choose to die.
With words of love and hearts of flame
Bear to the lost their Saviour's name.

XII.

We come, we come, prepared to fight,
  And prison'd souls unbind;
To win to glorious realms of light
  The wanderer and the blind.

XIII.

Oh! the bright day when, from His throne,
The King of Kings shall bless, and own,
  And call His chosen home;
And recompense each labour done,
Each passion borne, each convert won,
  With endless bliss to come.

XIV.

Though far away, our brothers still ye are,
Friends of our heart, associates in our prayers.
When on your God ye bend your raptured eyes,
What time ye lift the priceless Sacrifice,
Think ye on friends at home, and say, "O Lord,
Loved be Thy Name, Thy Majesty adored;
Thine is our heart, our blood, our being's breath;
Thine is our all in life, and Thine in death!"
AMEN.

ST. JOSEPH'S COLLEGE FOR FOREIGN MISSIONS.

The College Building Fund.

On Tuesday, the 29th of June, 1869, being the Feast of St. Peter and St. Paul, on a bright summer's day, a little procession, chanting litanies, closed by the Archbishop of Westminster carrying a relic of St. Peter the Apostle, was seen winding its way through pleasant fields to a rising ground not very far from the Mill-hill railway station. There it paused; and after a few words of prayer, the First Stone was laid of the First Missionary College in England.

The work for which we have been pleading for these last few months is, then, fairly begun; but only a small portion of the sum necessary for its completion has yet been raised.

This arises partly from the subject being little known, and partly from the prevalent idea that both men and money are too much needed in England to spare either for such a work. For our present requirements about £6000 or £8000 may suffice. This is not a large sum to ask for such a purpose, if we reflect on the £157,000 collected this year by the Protestant Church Missionary, the £177,000 by the Wesleyan Missionary, and the £200,000 by the British and Foreign Bible Societies. Yet this is all that we require in order to build a College which shall be the basis of operations for St. Joseph's Foreign Missionary

Society of the Sacred Heart. We are the possessors of between forty and fifty acres of freehold land, on which there is, in every respect, an admirable building site. A certain number of burses are already founded, so that the permanency of the work may be considered secured. In answer, therefore, to the somewhat selfish objection already alluded to, I would remark that, as to the men, those who have a vocation for the Foreign Missions would not stay at home: and that as to the means, the Archbishop has spoken, on three separate occasions, in terms which admit of no reply.

" It is because we have need of men and means at home that I am convinced we ought to send both men and means abroad." " In exact proportion as we freely give what we have freely received, will our works at home prosper, and the zeal and number of our priests be multiplied." And again, another person speaks : " This is the test and the measure of Catholic life amongst us. The missionary spirit is the condition of growth, and if the faith is to be extended at home, it must be by our aiding to carry it abroad. To say that we are overwhelmed with local claims and with home wants, and that the money expended for the Foreign Missionary College had better be spent on the spiritual destitution at our own doors, is the most shallow and the most miserable of delusions."

Let me ask, then, are there none among those who read this appeal burning with zeal for the salvation of 200,000,000 of heathens subject to the British flag ?—for the 600,000,000 or 900,000,000 of heathen and infidels who are said to people the largest portion of the globe? Are there none who will take up the cause of the most miserable and neglected beings upon the earth, make it their own, and fly with generous alms to their assistance? It is certain that whatever you may do for this Foreign Missionary College will return upon you and upon your country with interest, fifty, ay, a hundredfold. The very gold and silver that you give, the generosity, the zeal, the pure and disinterested love with which you give them, will return to you, be sure of it, with the certainty of a divine law of grace and charity, in an outpouring flood of gifts and graces upon yourselves, your homes, and the country which has reared you.

HERBERT VAUGHAN,

St. Joseph's College, Mill Hill, Hendon,
London, N.W.

July 15, 1869.

Subscriptions for the "College Building Fund" and for the "Education Fund" to be sent to the Very Rev. Herbert Vaughan, St. Joseph's College, Mill Hill, Hendon, N.W.; or to the Translator of this Life of "*Théophane Vénard*," Lady Herbert, 38, Chesham Place, London.

THE END.

www.ingramcontent.com/pod-product-compliance
Lightning Source LLC
Chambersburg PA
CBHW031819230426
43669CB00009B/1198